T0359596

Wakefield Press

Australian Rural Entrepreneurs

Raised in a small business family in Central Victoria, Kerry Anderson is founder of the *Operation Next Gen Program*, working with rural towns across Australia encouraging them to look at existing landscapes with fresh eyes and to adapt to change.

In 2017 Kerry was invited to Kansas City by the Kauffman Foundation to represent Australia and share best practice in building collaborative entrepreneurship ecosystems with fellow practitioners. In 2018 she was recognised with the inaugural 8point8 Regional Australia Innovation Ecosystem Leader Award and named a Top 50 Australian Regional Agent-of-Change. Her two adult children have learnt from their mother, establishing successful rural-based businesses.

www.kerryanderson.com.au

By the same author

Entrepreneurship: It's Everybody's Business

Australian RURAL ENTREPRENEURS

Redefining the Future

Kerry Anderson

Wakefield
Press

Wakefield Press
16 Rose Street
Mile End
South Australia 5031
www.wakefieldpress.com.au

First published 2021

Edited by Julia Beaven, Wakefield Press
Typeset by Michael Deves, Wakefield Press

ISBN 978 1 74305 814 5

A catalogue record for this
book is available from the
National Library of Australia

For Bryce and Elise
who have bravely taken the leap of faith and are wonderful role models
for their children Monique, Phoebe, Amarli and Ava.

And to all the courageous and inspiring entrepreneurs who are forging
new opportunities and reinvigorating businesses in rural Australia.

One initiative and business at a time, you are strengthening our rural
communities and redefining the future.

Contents

Foreword

If you are considering starting a business, or are already in business, this book is an essential read.

Over many years Kerry Anderson has ventured into rural areas to shine a light on amazing diverse entrepreneurs and businesses. There is no hard-and-fast rule for success, but we can all learn from each other and it is important that we keep learning in order to remain viable. As Kerry keeps reminding us, none of us can be complacent.

In this book you will read about the great achievements as well as the roadblocks that entrepreneurs and rural businesses encounter along the way.

We appreciated Kerry's belief in us as we worked to establish Bakery on Broadway and create a vibrant business to benefit our hometown of Wycheproof. Her stories of other rural businesses across Australia have helped us to build our knowledge and consider opportunities and challenges that may not otherwise have occurred to us.

Very few rural business owners have a formal qualification, but we are resourceful and have accumulated valuable knowledge and experiences. We are also proud of what we have achieved, not only for ourselves but for our community. Sharing our stories and helping each other to thrive in a rural business gives ideas and strength to others to do the same.

Thank you, Kerry, for believing in rural businesses and the people who drive them. We are a diverse lot and love our rural towns. We are determined to see our communities thrive and defy the all-too-common trend of a declining population and slow death.

Entrepreneurs and small businesses play a major role in the future of our rural towns, which is why this book is so important.

Ann Durie
Bakery on Broadway, Wycheproof

Preface

'There has never been a better time to become a rural entrepreneur.' I wrote these words just before coronavirus restrictions were imposed on Australia and they resonate even more strongly now.

In the digital age we have so many amazing tools at our fingertips, access to incredible amounts of information, and a global economy to tap into. Quite literally, no matter where we choose to live, the world is our oyster. Previously, rural businesses had to cope with the tyranny of distance; now the playing field is more on a level with businesses in the city.

Why wouldn't you want to live and work in a rural community? Currently those people who are designated as 'rural' comprise 10% of Australia's population. They enjoy the clean, green lifestyle without having to face a daily peak-hour commute. They have access to prime real estate at much lower prices, and infection is less likely to be transmitted during COVID-19, making them safer. They also play an important role, providing social and service hubs for our rural industries that produce food and fibre for our nation and the world.

Rural communities have always had their share of entrepreneurs. Previously isolated, they are now connected to the world and rapidly becoming home to a range of notable entrepreneurial businesses operating at a national and international level. With service industries on the rise not all business activities relate to a physical product or shopfront. Often referred to as the 'gig economy', more and more savvy people are becoming self-employed and contracting their services to the big corporates. In addition to talent, this requires business skills.

So, what is an entrepreneur? For some the perception of an entrepreneur is that of a young tech-savvy millionaire from Silicon Valley. A dated perception, I might add. In fact, it is anyone who sets up a business (or businesses), and in so doing takes on financial risks in the hope of making a profit. Far from being restricted to just start-ups, I believe that an entrepreneur is someone creating something new or doing something differently in a business setting. I would also argue that financial risk does not always apply, for instance in a digital world where capital investment can be minimal.

An important distinction between an entrepreneur and an innovator is that the former takes an idea to market. We all have great ideas but not all of us have what it takes to make a success of it. Sometimes that success might take multiple attempts.

In Australia the entrepreneurs quietly walk among us. They could be your neighbour, a family member, or a schoolmate. They might not willingly acknowledge the title and yet they exemplify it in many ways.

How do 'ordinary people' become entrepreneurs? Maybe you are already in business and looking for useful tips. Perhaps you are about to take that big leap of faith and would value some inspiration and insights from those who have gone before you. We all have something to learn from raw and authentic accounts. As a result of stories I've gathered from across rural Australia and my observations and experiences of being in small business, I've identified and explored ten distinctive attributes.

Entrepreneurs need to be **visionary** with an ability to look at existing landscapes with fresh eyes. They love a challenge and are exceptionally good at **problem solving**, often referred to as **innovators** and **opportunists**. While others may hesitate, they will grab an opportunity and run with it. They live and breathe initiatives that are their **passion**, often turning hobbies into **creative** enterprises. Hours will be spent diligently learning new skills and researching to the point where they become an expert in their field, despite the lack of a university qualification.

They are **courageous** and take not one but many calculated risks. They understand that every failure provides valuable learning and might take them a step closer to success. Unafraid of new ideas and not letting anyone or anything stand in their way, they are persistent and **determined**.

When faced with uncertainty, such as during the recent COVID-19 restrictions, they are **agile** and adaptable, moving on to new opportunities and new ways of working. They understand the value of **collaboration** and community. Most of all they *do* it, not just dream it and talk about it. All of the rural entrepreneurs in this book have taken control of their own destiny.

While not keen on seeking attention, rural people are generous in sharing their knowledge. Some of these stories are recent, others were written some years ago. Not all have gone to plan. Regardless, they all have something of value to share and I do hope that you are as inspired as much as I have been.

Kerry Anderson

2020

Visionary

Far from being fortune-tellers, those successful in business have an ability to look at a blank canvas and imagine what could be. Likewise, they can look at an existing business and imagine it taking a new direction or operating in a new way. They clearly know where they are heading even if they're not sure how they are actually going to get there!

Articulating your vision can be daunting, but it is essential, particularly when you need to enlist the help of partners and investors.

> 'You need to be able to communicate your ideas in a form that council and trades people can understand, you can't just have a vision in your head.'

An ability to look at existing landscapes with fresh eyes and to find new uses for old buildings forms the basis of Phil McConachy's experiences at The Mill Castlemaine. It's a fascinating story about how – by default – he became the owner of 9000 square metres of industrial buildings ranging in vintage from 1875 to 1996.

> 'Because our goal has always been to go organic, we were able to deal with everything that came up along the way.'

The Comiskeys speak about how empowering it was to write down their vision, to go organic on their Queensland cattle property, and for it to become a reality. David talks about the satisfaction of ticking off one small task at a time.

> 'I knew what I wanted to do but not how to do it.'

Ever dreamed of starting a business? Suzanne Carroll in Central Victoria woke up one morning and told her husband that she was going to start a business called Cool Clutch. And she did!

'Russia was high risk, but the turnover got us through the drought.'

An eight-year drought brought many companies based in agriculture to their knees, but Grizzly Engineering always has its eye on the horizon and targeted an overseas market to stay afloat during this difficult time.

'I saw a gap in the education system.'

And then there is the inspiring Wil Massara, founder and CEO of Youth Leadership Academy Australia. How refreshing to find such vision in a 15-year-old student!

Their vision is strong, but the execution remains fluid. Life in business is always full of interesting twists and turns.

The Mill Castlemaine

Phil McConachy, The Mill Castlemaine

Hailed as the latest vibrant and exciting tourist destination of Central Victoria, The Mill Castlemaine is providing inspiration to others in rural towns wanting to breathe a new lease of life into their old industrial sites. But, be warned, it's not a task for the faint hearted.

Often large industrial buildings struggle to find a new purpose and can present more challenges than are evident to the naked eye. Castlemaine's former Woollen Mill, dating back to 1875 and ravaged by fire on at least two occasions, fits perfectly into this category.

When the old mill site came up for tender in 2013, it was fortuitous that it caught the eye of farmer and stay-at-home dad Phil McConachy. Phil and his partner Ronnie Moule, a local general practitioner, were keen for an alternative income to their sheep farm, significantly destocked in the continuing dry conditions. They were searching for land to establish a potential self-storage business. While considerably larger than required, they saw the potential of the mill site. 'At first we thought it was too big but let's have a go,' says Phil. 'We saw the potential for a market of some kind, worked out some rental estimates, and took it from there.'

With the aid of a building valuer and town planners they put together a bid. As fate would have it, the tender was initially awarded elsewhere but after the buyer defaulted it came back to the McConachys. They were soon owners of 26,000 square metres of real estate with 9000 square metres of industrial buildings, some from the 1870s.

During the tender process Phil had spotted the owners of a local café and coffee roasting business checking out the site for a potential expansion of their business. He approached them for a chat. It was not long before they had their first tenant signed up, a core one at that, but there was still a long way to go.

Working with council has been an integral part of the process. With such a high-profile site Phil says they have been determined to 'keep squeaky clean' despite the many stories of how slowly councils can move, and of those who get started and get approval afterward.

'After a lot of negotiation with the local council we got an overall planning permit for the site, but it has been a bit of a regulatory nightmare,' admits Phil. One of the many hidden surprises was when the entire fire hydrant system had to be upgraded from 80 mm to 100 mm pipes – even though they already had double the flow and triple the water pressure required by the regulations.

'There is no negotiation with regulations; it's just black and white,' shrugs

Phil. 'On reflection, if we'd engaged an architect in the first place it could have highlighted some of these issues but then we would not have bought the site.'

With 80% of the site leased to a mix of food and hospitality vendors, manufacturers, and retail outlets by 2016, Phil says progress has grown organically into a vibrant hub.

While his star tenants, Edmund and Elna Schaerf, took charge of converting the space beneath the iconic chimney into the now popular Das Kaffeehaus, Phil looked after the rest of the site. 'We waited for the tenants to arrive and then constructed the spaces to meet their needs. Some have been start-ups, others have expanded from a home business to a commercial site, or just needed a bigger space to grow their business.'

A secondary consent application is submitted to council for each new tenant. 'New tenants who fit into the industrial zone can come in without council approval, but we consult anyway,' says the ever-cautious Phil.

Initially frustrated by council's limited staffing and delayed responses from the planning department, the relationship has improved with time, especially when the head of department noticed emails being sent by Phil at 4.30 in the morning. 'We now have a system in place and are getting better at it,' he is pleased to report.

Drawing on his previous skills as a fitter and turner and owner of an earthmoving construction business, Phil has supervised all the works on site. Numerous trades, the majority of which are local, have been contracted for the major works and two carpenters and a labourer continue to be engaged on a permanent basis.

Having survived the stress of getting the site operational and it rapidly gaining momentum as a tourist destination, Phil and Ronnie decided in late 2015 that it was time to give serious consideration to the branding.

'We wanted to honour the site as well as the town of Castlemaine, which gave us The Mill Castlemaine.'

His focus has now turned to attracting visitors from Melbourne.

'Cross promotion is very important with all the tenants and the whole town. We're not competitors, we're all in this together.'

Today, looking decidedly relaxed and rightfully satisfied with the results of their endeavours, Phil is comfortable reflecting on the challenges of the past three years. While an old bus parked at the back of the site still acts as his office, he now has the luxury of meetings over coffee in Das Kaffeehaus where the waiters know him by name.

Without a doubt, The Mill Castlemaine has reinvigorated the opportunities for small businesses and employment in the town at a time when inconsistent seasons are making farming difficult. As a parent of four boys aged 10 to 20, one of Phil's motivations is that The Mill Castlemaine will offer them the option to live and work in their hometown.

'If we'd known the complexities, we probably wouldn't have bought the site,' Phil says. 'But I'm glad we did,' he adds with a smile.

By early 2020, four years down the track, Phil's 'office' bus is still parked out the back of The Mill Castlemaine, but it appears that the site has gathered a life of its own.

'We have 41 businesses, the site is 93% tenanted, and currently only 2% more available for leasing,' Phil says. 'The latest business is a boutique cheese maker and cheese training facility opening midyear.' I don't tell him I've already found the chocolate makers!

The website lists a wide array of businesses – food, vintage, studios, workshops, think tanks and online – as part of the ever-growing precinct. When I catch up with Phil in February, between 12,000 and 15,000 people are visiting The Mill Castlemaine each month, a great success story. By the end of March, coronavirus restrictions have come into force and there are changes. 'The strength of this site is that it's not focused on just one thing,' Phil acknowledges. 'If we'd been just tourism it would have had a bigger impact.' While a quarter of the businesses onsite closed their doors, others have continued operating in some capacity. 'The café is still roasting coffee and the brewery is still brewing.'

Phil believes that community support has grown for their local manufacturer and internet business tenants. 'It will be quite interesting to see what happens in the next twelve months.'

Phil is negotiating with a number of tenants about rent relief and has had to push a few of his plans back while progressing others. Communicating with the bank was a priority. With reduced foot traffic on site, it has been a great opportunity to commence some 'not so tourism friendly' works. 'The timing has also worked well for our new cheese-maker tenant,' he points out. 'It's made their build much easier.'

With only four vacant spaces on site, Phil has continued to receive enquiries from prospective tenants during the restrictions. The 2018 installation of a 100 kW solar system (355 panels) was followed in March 2020 with a second installation, taking the site to a total of 200 kW. 'This powers half of our consumption.'

Media has also significantly changed. 'Our focus is on digital media as this is the way the world is going,' explains Phil. 'We've warned all our hard-copy media that we are progressively winding back the spend within their businesses.'

This inspiring business has grown from a disused factory site into a major tourist destination.

PHIL'S TOP BUSINESS TIPS

- Get town planners with experience in large projects – and preferably an existing relationship with your local council – involved right at the beginning.
- Go to your council and get their support before you spend money.
- Find a bank manager who understands business and develop a strong relationship with them.
- Communication is essential. You need to be able to communicate your ideas in a form that council and trades people can understand; you can't just have a vision in your head.

www.millcastlemaine.com.au

Melton

Rebecca and David Comiskey, Melton

Having an unrestricted dream and formulating a written plan can have far-reaching consequences, according to David and Rebecca Comiskey of Melton in Central Queensland.

In a harsh environment that swings from successive years of drought to a flood in the blink of an eye, it is hard to imagine how farming families continue to survive let alone run a successful business. Touring Melton, an 8500-hectare (21,000-acre) cattle property in Central Queensland, in 2016 I was privileged to witness the passion of David and Rebecca Comiskey as they paused to reflect on their achievements eight years into the implementation of a 20-year plan.

Nestled between the Drummond and Great Dividing ranges, Melton's brigalow soils are highly valued in terms of land prices. Fortunately for the Comiskeys, Melton was underdeveloped at the time of purchase so, although a huge investment, it was affordable for the young couple.

Drawing on modern farming techniques and networking with like-minded producers they have taken a new approach to farm management since purchasing the property. Entering the organic market, adopting a rotational grazing system, and maximising their herd management forms a three-pronged approach to their 20-year-plan. Closely monitoring and benchmarking their progress against previous years' performances has revealed that all three goals have progressed beyond their initial expectations.

Their first big decision was to go organic. The reason was quite simple, according to Rebecca. 'We decided to go with grass-fed organic cattle because that is what we like to eat ourselves.'

They were also aware that their capacity to remain viable with inflation and rising costs of inputs was limited. 'We don't have the scale that other properties have so we had to focus on quality rather than quantity,' explains David, who saw the greatest challenge was in believing they could do it. 'When you've been brought up controlling weeds with the use of chemicals, the hardest thing to do is to get rid of that paradigm in your head; to take a risk and go organic.'

Organic status dictates that any input has to be natural or organic for both stock and land. All new products are thoroughly researched and approved prior to ensure that they are compliant. Well experienced in conducting audits and monitoring other farm activities Rebecca picked up the annual reporting in her stride. It took just three years from application until they were certified to sell organic beef and the financial benefits were immediate. In 2016 organic beef was selling at around $7.20 per kilogram, as opposed to $4.50 per kilogram for mainstream beef.

David is quick to warn, however, that anyone wanting to fast-track organic status may encounter unexpected challenges. 'Because our goal has always been to go organic, we were able to deal with everything that came up along the way.'

At the crux of the Comiskey's planning is the introduction of rotational grazing. Five thousand acres are divided by electric fencing into four sections, all leading to a central water trough. Paddocks are rested according to the growth rate of the grass; 60 days in the growing period and up to 120 days in the non-growing, allowing time for the ground cover to replenish. 'Everything starts with the earth,' explains David. 'Healthy soils lead to healthy pastures which leads to healthy cattle and ultimately to healthy consumers.'

Good grazing practice stimulates growth of the native grasses and the introduced buffelgrass. 'The rotational grazing system is far more climate effective,' says Rebecca. 'For every one per cent increase in organic soil carbon achieved through good grazing land management, another 72,000 litres of water can be absorbed into the soils per hectare, making our property more resilient for the droughts that will always be a part of our business.'

Thanks to a Natural Resource Management grant they have been able to accelerate their plan with a quarter of the property already under the rotational grazing system. It has also given them the opportunity to make comparisons with other paddocks still on the set stock system. At a fence line separating a traditionally grazed paddock from a rotationally grazed paddock, the benefit is clear to see. 'We don't have to tell anyone, they can see for themselves,' says Rebecca.

Animal health is central to the rotational grazing system. Thanks to new and extensive water infrastructure powered by solar, the cattle have less than 750 metres to walk to water and are easily transferred from one section to another.

As part of their 20-year plan the Comiskeys have also focused on maximising management of their 1000 head of Brahman breeders, currently down in numbers due to recent drought conditions. The herd originated from David's father, giving them a great start.

'Genetics and genomics will help our rate of improvement and are important tools to help us achieve our breeding goal of well-adapted, high-eating, quality grass-fed beef,' says Rebecca. 'We are focused on providing what the consumer wants to eat.' Effectively they have increased the productivity of their breeding cows by introducing seasonal mating so that calves are born when rain is predicted, and pasture nutrition is best to assist the lactating cow.

'Each decision we make is weighed up both financially and ecologically,' Rebecca adds. 'For example, we're not rushing to restock cattle after the recent drought even though we've just had unexpected rain. It's good to let things recover. We believe there is a huge link with profitability and good ground cover or land management.'

Chatting with David and Rebecca it becomes evident that they also value their personal time to participate in sports such as barefoot waterskiing, a pastime that has taken them as far as the national titles. They engaged a farm hand, so ease of management has been a high priority while introducing their three new strategies to the business. Rebecca produces her mobile phone to demonstrate. Water storage, electric fences, and even rainfall can be monitored from afar.

It goes without saying that none of this has been easily achieved and it is no surprise that, a three-year drought aside, accessing capital and managing debt have been their two major challenges.

A schoolteacher by training, Rebecca is quick to pay credit to David's business acumen, which was fine-tuned during his ownership of an earthmoving business and investment in real estate. Her skills in monitoring and report writing have become equally valuable to the business.

In dealing with debt, they have closely monitored their progress. Regularly supplying their bank with budgets to actual results and yearly financials has helped establish a strong relationship and negotiate the tough drought years that would normally present lots of hard questions from financial partners.

'We didn't wait to be asked,' explains Rebecca. 'We knocked on the bank's door and kept giving them information.' She started with solid budgeting and compiling reports to help understand how they were travelling. This, however, still wasn't enough to satisfy her need to confirm they were making positive progress. Benchmarking against their own performance was the next step. 'That was a good business decision. Even the auditing for our organic status and monitoring of our pasture growth has been good for our business. We know how we are performing at all times. It's exciting.'

David believes that investing in their management skills has been a key to their success. They started by both completing an investment course to help them negotiate their finance and invest off farm to help droughtproof their business. Then they joined Resource Consulting Services, a business group of like-minded property owners that helped them further develop their 20-year plan. He was stunned with the power of simply putting down a dream in writing. 'I didn't believe how suddenly a wishlist can be ticked off and achieved.'

The group also helped them access resources that would have otherwise remained unknown. By matching a Queensland Rural Adjustment Authority Loan to help fund a Natural Resource Management Project, they were able to accelerate their plan. 'We went a bit bigger than we had planned but it was too good an offer to pass up,' says David. The result was 51 kilometres of polyurethane piping and 45 kilometres of fencing towards their rotational grazing infrastructure.

Both David and Rebecca are sitting on a number of industry and natural resource management groups. Joining is a no-brainer according to David. 'Before that we were just bumping along and inventing our own stuff. You meet so many like-minded people and share many great ideas.'

Changing the perception of their industry is another goal they both share. 'We like to think that we are custodians of the land,' says Rebecca, who has a number of family members recognised in the Stockman's Hall of Fame. 'It is our aim to leave our soils in better shape than how we found them.'

'Politics aside, it's important that city people come and visit to see exactly what we do and don't do,' says David. 'While we respect the old ways, we are open to trialling new ways.'

In 2019, Rebecca was named one of 17 Nuffield Scholars. This exciting achievement took her on a learning journey across Australia and the world.

Her focus was to investigate modern technologies that can be incorporated into beef production systems to increase the rate of genetic gain and enhance key profit drivers such as fertility, market compliance and production efficiencies.

'Selecting the best bulls to fulfil our herd-breeding objectives was my clear reason for applying for a Nuffield Scholarship,' she says. In October 2019 she was still enjoying the benefits as one of a group of International Nuffield Scholars attending the United Nations Committee on World Food Security Meeting in Rome. 'I may feel like a fish out of water,' says Rebecca, 'but our farms are influenced by discussions that occur at this level.'

From my perspective, agriculture's future is in good hands if this enterprising couple is any indication.

THE COMISKEY'S TOP BUSINESS TIPS:

- Dream big and have a plan.
- Maintain a good relationship with your bank manager, accountant and solicitor.
- Surround yourself with like-minded people.
- Access good advice and training.
- Be open to new ideas.

Cool Clutch

Suzanne Carroll, Cool Clutch

Ever dreamed of starting a business? Suzanne Carroll of Gisborne in Central Victoria woke up on 30 October 2015 and told her husband that she was going to start a business called Cool Clutch selling 'cool by nature and cool by name' handbags for women. And she did. True story!

One of the fastest growing sectors of entrepreneurs is that of middle-aged women, and you can't go past Suzanne of Cool Clutch for inspiration. Having left her previous marketing work in the corporate sector for health reasons, Suzanne had been searching for an idea.

'I was too young to retire and too old to be employable. I wanted to sell something online so I could stay home in my PJs,' she laughs.

Nothing could be further from that vision. Instead of languishing at home in her PJs she has found herself totally out of her comfort zone, drawing down on her house mortgage to fund the start-up, travelling overseas to negotiate with manufacturers, diving into the alien and expensive world of patents, entering and winning a Pitchfest, and becoming the very visible public face of her unique product. It has been a steep learning curve since waking up with her Cool Clutch dream.

Suzanne understands the benefit of sharing her journey to help others. She attends as many business conferences and networking events as possible. 'I'm always learning by listening to others,' she explains. 'Everybody I listen to generates an idea.'

Not one to sit around, Suzanne registered the domain name 'Cool Clutch' the very first day inspiration hit. It may seem impulsive, but the idea had been bubbling away since she had seen a cooler bag that stored wine on its side instead of in the usual upright position. She noted there wasn't one available in Australia. Her idea was to create stylish handbags that could also discretely store and keep cool wine, lunches and even medications that deteriorate in high temperatures. The patented distinction is a removable pocket that sits within the handbag.

'I knew what I wanted to do but not how to do it.'

Suzanne contacted 32 manufacturers via China's Alibaba website. She followed up those who spoke good English. Three were shortlisted before Suzanne met with them in Hong Kong. After selecting one they worked together on the design. Suzanne paid 30% upon placing the order, and a further 70% when the first 2500 handbags were ready to be shipped. It should have been an exciting day when the container arrived in Melbourne, but it turns out that some manufacturers like to cut corners and many of the initial order were faulty.

With the benefit of hindsight, Suzanne would advise others to do it differently. 'Yes, good English and being contactable by Skype is crucial, but I would tour the factory before committing to a contract and would not allow the products to be shipped out of China without first being checked by a quality agent.'

With a sample of what she wanted to achieve and a list of questions to ask, Suzanne returned to China in August 2016 to negotiate with a new manufacturer and tour their factory, plus engage a quality agent. Thankfully it was a much better outcome this time round.

Another valuable lesson has been to scale back the designs and colour choices. 'At one point I had 83 different handbag designs and colours,' Suzanne admits, 'but I'm scaling back to just three styles with a total of about 25 handbags in total. I've learned not to listen to everybody because some ideas just don't sell.'

Obviously, a website is crucial for an online business. It took Suzanne three attempts and over a year to get a site that she is happy with. 'Your biggest investment is your shopfront. Don't go with the first *special offer* on a website design you see advertised on social media,' she advises. Again, she learned a valuable lesson and researched who had the skills to do the work to her satisfaction. Once established she was able to look after the website herself.

A Facebook community of 4500 people has become a useful marketing tool for Cool Clutch's direct sales. 'I'm self-taught in social media,' Suzanne admits and loves the fact that she can drill down into demographics when boosting posts for as little as $20. She has also learnt the distinctions between different platforms. 'When I'm on Facebook I talk like I do to my girlfriends, but when on Linked In, it is more business.' But she finds it is word of mouth that generates the most sales. 'My biggest marketing is customers talking to their friends.'

Finding wholesalers for Cool Clutch has been another trial and error process. She began by attending the major gift and homeware expos but, having such a unique product, has realised that it is more effective to research the demographics and visit the stores. While Suzanne looks after sales in Victoria, she also has an agent in New South Wales, and is currently seeking agents for Queensland and South Australia. A recent visit to the Barossa Valley revealed that wineries are a great fit for her products.

Patenting the Cool Clutch concept worldwide is another significant investment that started within weeks of the new business being created. 'Looking at my initial decisions, they were more about convenience,' Suzanne says. 'I googled Patent Attorneys and found one in a location I was familiar with. I liked him but he turned out to be very expensive.'

More recently Suzanne has benefited from working with a business mentor who has helped her to understand her weaknesses and improve her business decision-making. 'Useful tips like learning to allocate a code word to specific marketing campaigns allows you to monitor the return on investment,' says Suzanne. Like every seasonal business she is also looking to overseas markets to 'follow the sun'.

Entering and winning a Bendigo Pitchfest in November 2016 gave Suzanne a great confidence boost, as did being named in the Australian Top 50 People in eCommerce in early 2019. 'It's nice to be recognised,' she admits.

Working from home has probably turned out a little differently than Suzanne imagined. With grown-up children who have left home, it has been easier to reallocate rooms to the business. The dining room is now the board room, the study is an office for Suzanne and a part-time employee, and the garage is used for picking and packing.

'We don't have anyone come to dinner anymore,' she smiled. 'We go out.'

When coronavirus hit in 2020, her trips to the wine regions were curtailed and the board room became a great place to do jigsaw puzzles. 'As expected, sales have completely died, no one needs a handbag when they stay home.'

Despite the restrictions, Suzanne kept busy. Shopify is proving to be a much more satisfactory online retail platform. Cellarbration liquor is trialling sales of Cool Clutch bags instore. She participated as one of 50 mentors in The Hack Games held in June. Like all good entrepreneurs, she also gave thought to how she can drop-ship jigsaw puzzles as a sideline before the restrictions lifted. For those not familiar with drop-shipping, it is a supply chain management system where the sales are handled by the retailer and goods are directly shipped to the customer by the manufacturer or another party.

If Suzanne has one more dream, it is to grow the business to a level where she can build a new office and warehouse with a childcare centre so more women are empowered to work.

Now that's a cool dream!

SUZANNE'S TOP BUSINESS TIPS:

- Engage a quality agent if you are manufacturing overseas.
- Get a business mentor to get you started.
- Network with other businesspeople.

  www.coolclutch.net

Grizzly Engineering

Kurt Poltrock, Wendy McAllister and Skye Poltrock, Grizzly Engineering

Who said manufacturing is dead in Australia? While it can be challenging in a global marketplace and extended dry seasons, Grizzly Engineering is living proof that long-term success is possible. Their ground-breaking technology is made in Swan Hill from start to finish and they survived the 2002–2010 drought years with a bold initiative.

It's an exciting day when I catch up with Grizzly's three company directors in Swan Hill. This innovative business established in 1983 has such a great reputation and I'm very grateful to spend time with Wendy McAllister and her two sons, Kurt and Skye Poltrock.

With Australia's wages significantly higher than our agricultural competitors in Canada and the United States it has become difficult for some Australian companies to compete in a global market. But when it comes to competing with cheaper imports in the domestic marketplace Skye, who oversees sales and marketing, has no qualms about the reason for their continued success. 'It's all about quality manufacturing and backing it up with service. We listen to our customers.'

Kurt, who has stepped into the role of General Manager since Wendy retired from day-to-day operations, adds that they have invested heavily in technology and design to meet customer needs and grow their sales. Their growing list of equipment meets a wide range of needs, including no-till cropping and vineyard maintenance.

Getting the right employees is also crucial according to Kurt. Ninety per cent of Grizzly's employees are sourced locally, and adult apprenticeships are becoming more prevalent. 'In-house training works well for us. We are prepared to put on unskilled people with the right attitude.'

When I suggest we get a photograph of all three directors together, Kurt leads us out on to the factory floor where a startled young man pauses from his welding to pose with the group. 'I wanted you to see that we build our machinery from start to finish,' he explains.

The factory floor is also where Kurt started his working life with the company in 2000. He started working in various roles on the assembly line, earning his welding certificate, and spending time in stores to get a good overview of the company. At the time he became General Manager, employee numbers grew from 27 to 42, indicating that he is doing well in the leading role.

Kurt is strong on process. 'Everything needs a procedure,' he explains. 'Get it on paper and it makes it easier for everyone.' He is a great fan of a Manufacturing Resource Planning (MRP) system that controls their production and inventory as well as integrating accounts and payroll. 'It's a very powerful product and I can't understand why other manufacturing companies don't use these tools. We have full control of our costings.'

He also believes that procedures keep all team members accountable. 'We have good processes in place, so my job is really just to help everyone else do their job,' he explains.

Skye recognises that he has different strengths to Kurt. 'I'm quite good at talking to customers,' Skye says. 'I love my job. There are so many variables. No two farmers want the same outcome and I get great satisfaction from selling quality machinery to meet their needs.' Skye credits Kurt's strong management for continuing to keep the company on an even keel when everyone expects it to falter in such a tough marketplace.

I ask about the eight-year drought that saw many Victorian farms and businesses falter. 'We noticed a gradual decline in sales from 2002 onwards,' Kurt explains, acknowledging the irony of the drought officially ending with extended flooding across the region in 2010. Clearly, they had to do something different to survive in the years between. Looking for a new market turned out to be a saviour.

Through Wendy's involvement as Grizzly's representative with the Australian Tractor & Machinery Association, she developed a contact in Russia, which ultimately sold 50 units of their Field Boss and helped them through this difficult period. Skye had joined the company in 2008, the last two years of the drought, and quickly came to appreciate the hard work that Wendy and the senior managers had put in to ensure that Grizzly could survive and retain their employees. He also got to travel to Russia. Despite the challenges of doing business in a foreign country, three sales became 50 and Grizzly Engineering staff were kept busy filling the orders. 'Russia was high risk, but the turnover got us through the drought,' Kurt acknowledges.

It is no surprise that Grizzly remained positive when 2019 presented more drought conditions. 'We focus on the things we can control, our business and staff, to ensure we can remain standing during the tough times as well as the not so tough times,' said Skye. Fortunately, agriculture continued to operate as an essential industry during coronavirus.

Like all good businesses, success hinges on meeting your customer's needs, adapting during tough times, and constantly looking toward the future.

www.grizzlyag.com.au

Youth Leadership Academy Australia

Wil Massara, Youth Leadership Academy Australia
(Courtesy West Australian Newspapers Limited)

Catching up with the much-in-demand Wil Massara, CEO and Founder of Youth Leadership Academy Australia, in 2018 took some doing. We eventually arranged to meet in the central park at Collie in the south-west region of Western Australia.

School had finished for the day and 15-year-old Wil was up for a spearmint milkshake. I ordered a double-shot espresso as I tried to understand what was driving this ambitious young man.

Is this his first business I ask?

'Well, it's my first legal business,' he admitted with a smile. Straightaway I'm intrigued ... and distracted. Where is this leading?

It turns out that Wil once ordered 100 pens from a promotional company but they failed to arrive on time, so he got them for free. Then he ordered another 100 pens and it happened again. To cut a long story short, Wil got 200 pens for free and sold them for $2 each, making him a cool $400 profit.

So, as this story has confirmed, Wil can immediately recognise an opportunity and grab it. Tick!

By now the milkshake is gone and I've barely started on my espresso. It's time to get down to business, his new legal one that is. The recent launch of the Youth Leadership Academy Australia has created much interest and Wil admits that he's also been interviewed by the local newspaper. 'Why has he started it?' is the question on everyone's lips.

'I saw a gap in the education system,' Wil explains. 'We're not being taught the skills we need for the future, only for the jobs of today and the past. Young people are being trained to work for someone else and not focusing on the necessary life skills to be successful.'

Wil's vision is to provide one and two-day conferences, seminars and workshops, especially for young people aged 15 to 18 years, with nationally renowned speakers and life strategists. The very first Western Australian Youth Conference is being planned for the 28 August and tickets are priced at the incredibly low price of $20 per person.

'I need 77 people to break even,' he confirms when I ask about his budget. Even so I am still dubious, until he reveals that he is seeking corporate sponsorship to keep the costs down for students. For instance, the speaker, Anna Richards, is flying to Perth and speaking pro bono as a favour to Wil.

Never one to miss an opportunity, Wil quickly adds, 'If anyone would like to sponsor the Youth Leadership Academy Australia, please email me at ylaaus@gmail.com.'

There could be many who doubt Wil's capacity as a student to establish a

Wil Massara in Melbourne at a sell-out YLAA forum in March 2020

successful business, however, he has had plenty of help along the way. Let's start with his mum, who dropped him off for the interview. I suggest that he may have to put her on staff, but he is quick to dismiss that notion. Secretly I hope she reads this interview and commences negotiations!

The Collie & Districts Community Branch of Bendigo Bank sponsored him to attend the Magic Moments event for young achievers in 2016. Through the Magic Moments network Wil connected with his mentor, Andrew Daley from Singapore, who helped him with a business plan. He has also partnered up with a fellow delegate, 19-year-old Maddy Hedderwick, who has taken on the role of Operations Manager as she works her way through a double major in Management and Sports Science at university.

Utilising his own technology skills, Wil has established the business website. In short, he paid $88 to register the business and $100 to set up the website. Hmm, I can see where the $400 profit from his first 'business' has come in useful.

Time management is essential. 'I have a very strict schedule,' Wil reveals. 'Set times for study, personal development and business.' I assume this interview falls into the business timeslot. Wil comes from a business-orientated family and everything he is doing at school is aimed at building his business skills. When I first spoke to him in 2018 he was studying Business Management and undertaking a Certificate III in Business.

'My aim is to benefit society,' Wil explains, 'but I also want to have a profitable business. If you only have enough money for yourself then you are selfish.' That is probably the best explanation I've heard of why a business should be profitable, and I heard it from a 15-year-old student in rural Australia! Maybe our future is brighter than I thought.

Fast forward to 2020 and Wil has predictably failed to achieve a Western Australian Certificate of Education in Year 12. He's 17 years old, working for himself, and doesn't care!

He has also done what he said he was going to do. He successfully launched the Youth Leadership Academy Australia in Perth in 2018. In the following months he took it to a national level, hosting a State Youth Leadership Conference in four cities with 272 students. These achievements earned him an International Young Philanthropist award.

In March 2020 the State Leadership Conference once again toured Perth, Adelaide, Sydney, Melbourne and Brisbane, with all events close to selling out. When coronavirus restrictions hit Wil seamlessly transferred his attention to running a series of Virtual Young Entrepreneurs Summits.

Nothing will stop this enterprising young man.

www.ylaaus.com

Courageous

Whether it is starting a business, taking on a business, changing the direction of a business, or starting over again when things don't go to plan, it takes courage. This is not someone else's investment, it is yours. Your life savings and sometimes your family's nest egg are being invested with no surety of the outcome. In time, this business is what hopefully generates enough profit to pay the mortgage and put food on the table. Chances are you will also have employees relying on you for the very same reasons. There are no guarantees. You can do all the research in the world but there is always that element of fear that it may not work out.

It takes courage to accept the setbacks and start over again when things do go terribly wrong. Just a series of little setbacks can make your heart sink on those tough days that we all experience at some time or other. But this is all part of the learning process and necessary in achieving success.

'I had lots of failures along the way but learnt from them all. Some lessons you pay a higher price to learn than others.'

Michelle Anderson-Sims can still recall her first $20 sale, which seemed such a huge milestone at the time, but five years on she is rightfully satisfied with Wine in a Glass's turnover that has reached six digits. This successful company has made its mark on the Australian wine and entertainment industries and is rapidly expanding throughout the world.

'Don't accept the first no.'

When Cohuna teenager Jenni Finn got a casual job in an orange-juice factory in the 1980s she had no idea that one day she would own that building and establish one of her hometown's most successful businesses in recent years.

'We had to sell everything we possibly could, including the family car, to fund it. We really jumped in the deep end.'

What do you do when you live in an isolated rural community and can't find shoes for your toddler? Well, if you're Andrea Harrison from Birchip, you start up your own online business, Kawaii Kids, importing children's shoes and clothing. Then you start manufacturing your own lines.

'My first Christmas present at Mount Mitchell was an 80-metre bore.'

When lifestyle becomes a priority how do you balance it with a viable business? Simon and Kate Tol are in the process of finding out, having recently taken ownership of the historic property Mount Mitchell near Lexton, in the north-west district of Victoria.

'As a mum without a paid job, I couldn't even get a credit card!'

The creators of Retro Respection, a quirky homeware, giftware and vintage lovers' shop in Collie, Western Australia, are an inspiration to all those young mums who may feel trapped at home.

Being in business requires great courage, as these stories of start-up businesses demonstrate.

Wine in a Glass

Michelle Anderson-Sims, Wine in a Glass

Managing Director of Wine in a Glass (WIAG), Michelle Anderson-Sims, is the first to admit that starting a business from an idea is a long hard learning process. 'I had lots of failures along the way but learnt from them all. Some lessons you pay a higher price to learn than others,' she says. She can still recall the first $20 sale, which seemed such a huge milestone at the time, but five years on she is rightfully satisfied with a turnover that has reached six digits. This successful company has made its mark on the Australian wine and entertainment industries and is rapidly expanding throughout the world.

When I first tried to catch up with this enterprising businesswoman in 2018, she came up with the best excuse ever. The Commonwealth Games were in full swing and WIAG had been contracted to be the sole provider of 250,000 glasses of Australian wine at the event. 'They've sold out,' Michelle told me over the phone and texted me photos of the extra pallets they were preparing for a dash to the venues.

I sat down at last with Michelle in February 2019 and was able to revisit her extraordinary story as well as get a hint about future developments. It was worth the wait. Even if you didn't get to the Commonwealth Games, chances are you've experienced this innovative product if you've attended a match at the GABBA or Etihad Stadiums or attended a Pink, Adele or Red Hot Summer Tour concert. Effectively, WIAG has captured the events market with premium Australian wines vacuum-sealed in food-grade, fully recyclable and reusable PET cups, which provide an excellent alternative to glass.

'We are filling a void,' explains Michelle. 'When you need to serve 5000 people in a 15-minute window, speed of service becomes critical. Our portion-controlled wine can help to address this, using our pre-packaged products.'

Even cinema, hospital, and aged-care facilities have recognised the value of WIAG products, which are approved for arthritis sufferers.

While some sales are made directly through their website, the majority are through distributors Australia and worldwide. Currently they are exporting to countries such as Malaysia, New Zealand, China, Japan, Korea and Columbia. With Michelle well versed in international trade, she is constantly extending this list.

The quality of the cups and the unique sealing process ensures that the products are tamper evident and have a long shelf life – 18 months for white wines, two years for red. After use they can even be recycled. I've tucked my sample cups away for my next bush picnic and Michelle tells me that customers have posted pictures on the WIAG Facebook page of lemon butter and jam in WIAG cups.

Touring the Echuca manufacturing plant, it becomes evident that this enterprise has required significant investment. Michelle obtained the exclusive intellectual property from France for use in Australia. It is an expensive exercise to bring a container of 140,000 Sims glass cups from France to Echuca. 'In-country logistics are a handicap to our business as we are some 2.5 hours from the port but we have factored these costs into our business model so we can maximise employment opportunities for local residents.'

Over a two-year period WIAG undertook and achieved accreditation for Hazard Analysis Critical Control Point (HACCP) certification. 'It's a big investment for a start-up,' Michelle admits, 'but a brilliant framework for our business and improved our production practices and quality output.' Make no mistake. This is big business happening in a rural setting.

If, like me, you thought Michelle came from a manufacturing or wine industry background, we are all mistaken. I ask how she reached this point and her story is inspiring.

First and foremost, Michelle is mother to four children ranging in ages from 14 to 22 years. It was during a family holiday in Europe that she first stumbled on the concept and realised the opportunity for the Australian market. To that point, with only a secretarial diploma to her credentials, she had been working in a series of senior management corporate roles that had earned her the reputation of being efficient, especially when facing challenges.

Discovering the wine in a glass concept in Europe was an opportunity for her to start her own business. Michelle admits that her first mistake was in starting out using a similar product from the USA. 'It was a failure because the market didn't like the wines produced in the United States.'

She quickly backtracked to the French manufacturers and designed her own fully recyclable and reusable PET 'Sims Cup' with the intention of filling them with premium Australian wines. She began by renting a portion of the premises of one of her wine suppliers, an Echuca-based vineyard. She made the decision to purchase the entire property as WIAG rapidly grew, tripling its sales each year.

In the early days of the business Michelle took advantage of a mentoring service. Getting the right team around her has been crucial and she is the first to say how lucky she has been. 'You have to surround yourself with positive people who share your passion and vision for the business.' A lot of young people, particularly those in their GAP year, gravitate to work with WIAG's core team who are committed to providing opportunities for skill improvement.

When it comes to marketing, Michelle admits that it is a handicap being a long way from Melbourne but says that LinkedIn and social media have helped the company to grow. 'You just have to be creative.'

It was a busy start to 2020 for WIAG. They sponsored the Southern 80 Ski Race and supplied wine to major concerts around Australia. Festival City Wines had started stocking their range, increasing their reach to the domestic marketplace. This rural company was ticking all the right boxes with a refreshed website, new branding, and a growing number of export destinations.

When coronavirus impacted on events and WIAG sales worldwide, Michelle quickly saw a demand for hand sanitiser products and an opportunity to keep her staff employed. Utilising her Chinese contacts to source raw materials, the new line complete with Happy Jack promotional posters was introduced in May.

WIAG pre-packaged wines will be especially welcome post COVID-19 with hygiene being carefully scrutinised. As events resumed in other states, Michelle was probably the only Victorian happy that the Australian Football League grand final was being played at the Gabba in Brisbane where she has a contract with the caterer! She is also grateful that COVID has levelled out the playing field for rural businesses. Instead of being asked to fly to capital cities for brief meetings with clients, she is now able to meet online and make better use of her time.

When it comes to advice for other business owners, Michelle has two key recommendations. 'Share the vision of your business with staff and, if you see an opportunity, grab it and run with it.'

www.wineinaglass.com.au

Factory and Field

Jenni Finn, Factory and Field (Courtesy Michelle Howard)

When Cohuna teenager Jenni Finn got a casual job in an orange juice factory in the 1980s she had no idea that one day she would own that building and establish one of her hometown's most successful businesses in recent years.

Visitors to Cohuna in northern Victoria often struggle to find the much-talked about Factory and Field store. Owner Jenni Finn is just a little embarrassed to admit that she has been too busy to organise the signage despite just celebrating their third anniversary. 'It's still on the to-do list,' she admits.

Housed in an old butter factory building from the 1880s and used for a multitude of purposes over the years, Factory and Field is tucked away on the back road to Leitchville in an industrial estate. It's not exactly where you'd expect to find a popular homewares and gift store – and that is part of its charm.

Jenni's father purchased the old factory site in 1991 to expand his Cohuna Steel business and when he retired in 2012 Jenni and her husband offered to take it on. Looking at the building with the artistic eye of a photographer one can understand why Jenni found it appealing, with its massive concrete walls and corrugated-iron roof framed with steel girders. With a three-storey-high ceiling and extensive natural lighting from the old factory windows high in the roofline, she essentially had a blank canvas to work with.

But, of course, it wasn't that simple. Jenni was too busy supporting her husband with his auto electrical business and raising three children to do more in 2012. For a while she used a room in the factory as a part-time photographic studio while dreaming of what else it could be. That day finally arrived in 2013. 'The kids were older and it was finally time to do something on my own,' says Jenni. Profit was another factor. 'The commercial rental rate was extremely low, around $600 per month,' she explains. 'I knew I could get a better return than that on our asset.'

With the encouragement of a supportive and resourceful husband she made the plunge. Factory and Field was born in a bit of a rush; three months to be exact. Jenni made the decision in July, purchased stock at a trade fair in August and opened in September 2013. Her idea on what to sell was simple. 'I'd only stock things that I'd have in my own house and, fortunately, what I like suits the building.' A name for the business was also straightforward. 'Factory and Field had a country feel to it.'

What didn't come so easily, however, was finance. While their bank had been happy to support the purchase of the building, it wasn't prepared to finance the business. Undeterred Jenni used her personal credit card to purchase minimal stock and gave the building a bit of a tidy up.

On opening night around 130 curious locals came and devoured her entire stock in a few hours. Jenni was both stunned and relieved. Over the next three days of trading she spent her time explaining why stock had sold out and people were only too happy to come back the following week when they had restocked.

Three years on and Factory and Field is continuing to grow and evolve. Additional rooms have been opened up to house a café and a Christmas themed section. What started as self-serve coffee with an urn grew into a fully serviced café. 'As with everything around here it just gets bigger as we talk about it,' Jenni smiles. And she has the space to do it, with more of the four-acre site awaiting her vision. A function room and holiday accommodation units are just two ideas on the drawing board.

And the customers keep coming from even further afield. 'Car loads drive from places as far away as Heathcote and Mildura to browse the shop and have lunch in Cohuna before driving home again,' says Jenni. 'People will travel for something different and to be entertained.'

Like everything else Jenni has applied to her business, the marketing has been kept simple. Facebook is her number-one method of advertising and, best of all, it's free. 'I looked at other sites that worked well and used my photography skills to make the posts interesting.' One of her monthly 'Like and Share prize' postings was viewed over 60,000 times, which helps explain the geographical spread of her customers. Word of mouth has taken care of the rest and the shop is buzzing from Thursday through to Sunday each week, staffed by six employees.

Reflecting on the success of her business, Jenni concedes that growing up in a family business made her aware of the possibilities, however, it has exceeded her expectations. 'I had no time to have an expectation,' she admits.

She is also pragmatic. 'Yes, we would have liked $50,000 for fittings and to properly stock the store when we opened but we could only do what we could afford to do at the time. Sometimes your instincts are good.'

Shortly after we first spoke Jenni saw the potential in another vacant building, this time a former service station. Factory and Field Waffles opened in October 2017. With its more central location and drive-by traffic it made perfect sense to combine Factory and Field gift shop with the Waffles cafe. So, since 2019, the original Factory and Field building only opens for special exhibitions and festivals.

And then came the coronavirus in March 2020! 'We managed to stay open for takeaway but closed the shop,' Jenni says. Looking after their older employees was a priority and they continued to have four or five working each day. A bonus is that they decided not to open weekends. 'We've had weekends at home for the first time in eight years,' she exclaimed delightedly, but then admitted that most of that time off was spent working in the shop behind closed doors.

One of her projects has been to promote a line of 'forever flowers', with excellent sales for Mother's Day. 'It's always good to try something different. Now we have a section just for flowers in the shop.'

JENNI'S TOP BUSINESS TIPS:

- Don't accept the first 'no'.
- Fake it till you make it.
- Don't be afraid to learn as you go.
- Work in an area you enjoy.
- Work with people who enjoy the same work you do.
- Employ enthusiastic and friendly staff.
- Don't be afraid to make changes in your business when you find something is not working. Not everything needs to be set in stone.

  www.facebook.com/FACTORYANDFIELD

  www.facebook.com/factoryandfieldwaffles

Kawaii Kids

Andrea Harrison and family

What do you do when you live in an isolated rural community and can't find shoes for your toddler? Well, if you're Andrea Harrison from Birchip, you start up your own online business importing children's shoes and clothing. Then you start manufacturing your own lines, collaborate on a specialist baby range with selected retail stores, and introduce an upmarket point-of-sale system to cater for even more growth. And that's just in the first nine years!

It all began when Andrea, a young mother and wife of a dryland farmer, wrestled with the shoe dilemma.

'I started thinking that other parents in rural areas were experiencing the same issues,' says Andrea, who didn't just stop at sourcing shoes. After experimenting with eBay, in 2007 she launched her online business, Kawaii Kids, selling children's clothing and accessories imported from Japan, Korea and China. At this time online businesses in the rural sector were a rarity and hers won her a local business award, and, in 2011, a Victorian Regional Achievement & Community Award.

The business operated from the family home; clothes were stored in industrial containers in the backyard and a laptop on a small desk in the hallway acted as her business hub. Birchip's post office suddenly experienced a lot more throughput. Recognising she was on a winner, Andrea started planning for growth when she was barely 12 months into the business.

Much has been achieved in almost a decade since launching her business career. Her next step was to free up the family home by opening a retail store in Birchip. A few years later it was relocated to the larger regional city of Horsham. After being approached by a new shopping centre developer, Kawaii Kids then moved into the brand-new Gateway Shopping Centre in Horsham in prime position next to Target.

'I was aware that it takes people 18 months to change their shopping habits and our landlord helped in many ways to us get through that initial period in the shopping centre,' says Andrea.

During this time, she spent many days working in the store. This saved on wages but also gave her great insight into the shopping habits of customers.

'One big lesson I learned in retail was to stop listening to what people say and go with my gut, which is generally right,' she says. 'Shoppers are savvy now and compare your products with online prices. The big chain stores have copied a lot of the designer brands and saturated them online, making it hard for the smaller stores. My strategy is to stock brands that don't have a big online presence. It is my main point of difference.'

As part of that point of difference, Andrea has also started manufacturing her own line of children's clothing under the Curious Wonderland brand. This required her to take on a second lease when the adjacent store space became available. Removal of the dividing wall allowed staff to service both businesses. As always, Andrea put a lot of thought and research into her new venture, making the decision to establish a brand independent of Kawaii Kids so that each business could be sold separately in the future.

After being approached by one of her contacts in China about the possibility of manufacturing her own line of clothing, Andrea leapt at the opportunity, but it did come with challenges, the first being finance. Instead of buying a number of items off the rack she now had to commit to large quantities to make it viable. Without a credit history – she had self-funded all her business activities to date – the banks would not consider a business loan, despite her impressive cash-flow figures. It was a bitter lesson for someone who had worked hard to prove her worth in the business world. 'We had to sell everything we could, including the family car, to fund it. We jumped in the deep end.' Ironically, 12 months on with the new business proving its worth, the banks are finally starting to show interest.

The Curious Wonderland line was successfully launched at the Sydney Trade Show in February 2015, picking up 23 retailers on the spot. It was a huge relief to Andrea who had considered the possibility that her own children may have to wear these clothes forever!

Another challenge was the uncertainty of whether customers would like Andrea's designs. Based on her children's preferences (by now she had three) and following her gut instincts, Andrea sketched out her designs before passing them on to a graphic designer and pattern maker to prepare for the manufacturing stage. Attention to detail on the Pantone colours and interpretation of the smaller design details were crucial. Samples were scrutinised and evaluated by the ever-vigilant Andrea. 'I'm very fussy. What I'm doing is very different to what everyone else is doing. They're getting to know me,' she laughs.

As always Andrea relentlessly researched every aspect of manufacturing in China during the lead up. 'I just hopped online to do my research and joined retail groups on Facebook. I asked lots of questions about labelling and manufacturing,' says Andrea. 'You have to be aware that there are chemicals used in China that aren't allowed in Australia. It would be devastating to have it pulled up in Customs.'

Despite being a great success overall, there have been a few expensive lessons along the way. In Andrea's words, 'It's been a huge learning curve.' A line of denim clothing ordered through a separate manufacturer was delayed by extended Chinese holidays missing delivery for the winter season and resulting in cancelled orders.

'I remember driving down to the docks in pouring rain aware that I had just thrown $55,000 down the toilet despite putting my heart and soul into it,' Andrea admits. 'I learnt the value of staying with just the one production run.' She now understands the Chinese holiday system a bit better as well.

In her latest project manufacturing a range of baby clothes, Andrea has opted to minimise the risk by sharing the cost with seven other retailers who will get to exclusively stock the products. 'We've all agreed on the designs and are prepared to try it out. We don't have to commit to such high quantities when the order is split between seven of us. So far, so good.'

Andrea was strategic about who she invited into this collaboration, asking for expressions of interest through an online retail forum. Selected storeowners from Queensland, New South Wales, South Australia and Victoria have agreed to pool their ideas and knowledge.

With growth in mind Andrea has also committed to Retail Express, a point-of-sale system with the capacity to track inventory over multiple businesses, both in-store and online.

'It will bring everything together and allow me to oversee all my businesses from home.'

Balancing family and seasonal farm priorities has been an ongoing challenge for Andrea, who is grateful to have the support of her partner, Daniel. 'I've got so much I want to do,' she admits with a hint of frustration. 'My business is now contributing to the family income, which is a relief given the number of dry years we've had. It's good not to have all our eggs in the one basket. I just have to be flexible and fit in with Daniel when he's available to help out.'

With the arrival of their fifth child in 2018, one could be forgiven for thinking that Andrea has slowed down, but this appears not to be the case. Kawaii Kids continues to operate online with a healthy 22,000+ followers on Facebook. A VIP Kawaii Kids Club Facebook Page has also been introduced to showcase special offers through the physical storefront in Horsham. The Curious Wonderland brand is gaining traction across Australia.

Life is obviously busy for Andrea. How on earth does she do it? 'It is chaotic,' she laughs. 'I wish I was wired differently and could sit down and relax. I really envy people who can do that.'

Fortunately, with three trusted staff to run the two combined Horsham stores, Andrea has the flexibility of running the online sales and monitoring the store from her laptop on the kitchen bench. This came in particularly handy during coronavirus and home-schooling requirements.

It goes without saying that she never stops exploring new ideas. 'I research everything I want to do just in case I can do it one day,' she says with a hint of defiance.

ANDREA'S TOP BUSINESS TIPS:

- Be proactive and stay ahead of your competitors.
- Find a point of difference.
- Ask for referrals and interview other customers before committing to large cost items or services for your business.
- Understand overseas cultures and potential impact on your production and delivery processes.
- Research, research, research!

www.kawaiikids.com.au

Mount Mitchell Homestead

Kate Tol, Mount Mitchell Homestead

When lifestyle becomes a priority how do you balance it with a viable business? Simon and Kate Tol are in the process of finding out, having just 18 months ago taken ownership of the historic property Mount Mitchell near Lexton, in the north-west district of Victoria.

As a youngster living in Geelong, Simon Tol recalls driving along the Sunraysia Highway to visit his grandparent's farm at Donald. 'Two bachelors live there,' his father told him once as they passed Mount Mitchell, 'and they store their grain in the ballroom.'

While the grand house, built in 1861 and expanded in 1910, was hardly visible from the road, that bizarre story stuck in Simon's mind. It is hardly surprising that four decades later he and wife Kate were attracted by an advertisement in the *Weekly Times* seeking expressions of interest for the very same historic property, now reduced to 325 fertile hectares.

The timing was right. Simon had been running his own successful plumbing and construction business for 10 years, mainly in the commercial space, and was ready for a change. 'I hated the paperwork; having to be compliant, and the whole tender process,' he admits. 'You'd work hard, sometimes for three or four years at a time on a big job, and then have to spend a couple of years trying to get paid.'

Kate, who was the Head of Physical Education and Health at The Geelong College for 24 years, in addition to renovating various properties with Simon, was also ready for a new challenge. 'We both ran out of projects and were ready to do something else. Neither of us are good at sitting around.'

An inspection of Mount Mitchell revealed that the land was leased for cropping while the 27-room house, complete with 18 fireplaces and four hectares of gardens, had been lovingly restored over a 34-year period by Richard Salter. Richard, a successful New South Wales grazier with a past family connection to the property, had saved it from the previous bachelor farmers who only valued the land and allegedly slept in their car because it was warmer than the house and had a wireless.

'Everywhere we looked, we were amazed,' says Kate, recalling their first visit. 'We already had a picture-perfect home in Geelong, and we were looking for something unique.' Mount Mitchell hit the mark for them both, and they assured Richard they would make perfect custodians.

So strong were their instincts, an unconditional offer was made on the property immediately after their second inspection. A six-month settlement allowed them to realise their assets to meet the sale requirements and plan for their exciting move with the family.

Mount Mitchell Homestead

Lifestyle for them and their three children – Will aged 18, Sophie 16, and Harry 10 – has been an important component of their decision.

'We wanted our children to have the opportunity to be more hands on,' explains Kate. In other words, everyone is required to pitch in! Sophie is also raising seven calves in her own business enterprise. 'We're all involved in the local community and are loving country life.'

'We don't miss the hustle and bustle of Geelong at all,' confirms Simon, who has just been elected President of the Waubra Football Club following a term as vice-president.

'So, let's talk about your business plan for Mount Mitchell,' I suggest. Simon promptly informs me that they don't have one, but Kate is more forthcoming. Informal planning and bouncing ideas off each other is part of their daily life. 'We love living here but it still has to be viable. Richard, the previous owner, was very private. We have opened Mount Mitchell up to the community,' she explains. 'For the moment, we are focusing on farming produce, events, and accommodation.'

Making the transition from construction to farming could be considered a risk, however Simon has accumulated useful skills over the years. 'I got my wool-classing certificate in the 1990s and a few years ago we purchased 250 acres at Moonambel as a weekender and loved it so much that we purchased the adjacent farm,' he explains.

Simon is particularly grateful to their new neighbours at Mount Mitchell. 'They've been just wonderful with their advice and support.' His first challenge was to restore the 325 hectares previously planted with crops into pasture for prime lamb production. Fortunately, they already had sufficient farming machinery from the Moonambel property and Simon's construction equipment also came in handy.

Sheep are an important part of the property's history. Original owners, alongside assigned convicts, drove 48 merino rams down from Elizabeth Farm in New South Wales to Mount Mitchell in 1838. While the current homestead wasn't constructed until 1861, there were numerous shepherd huts and outbuildings to service the 8500 hectares. Mount Mitchell was established only three years after Melbourne. An early map of the district notes the Adelaide to Geelong Road, highlighting that Ballarat didn't exist at that time.

With the paddock-to-plate concept becoming increasingly popular worldwide, Simon and Kate were delighted to be introduced to Melbourne-based executive chef Ian Curley, who wants to stock their product in his restaurants. Not only their prime lamb but also the produce from their large kitchen garden. Kate has spent the first year of their property ownership shadowing the gardener of 17 years learning the ropes and has recently taken responsibility for maintaining the four hectares of gardens, with some help from contract gardeners.

'My first Christmas present at Mount Mitchell was an 80-metre bore,' she laughs. 'Installing an underground sprinkler system is next on my wish list.'

The Tol's value Mount Mitchell as their family home and the homestead is strictly off limits for events. They are concentrating on outdoor events, utilising the extensive garden spaces and historic outbuildings such as the National Trust-listed stable block.

'We are aiming for events at the exclusive end of the market,' Kate explains. 'We want to retain Mount Mitchell as a high-quality brand. It's a unique place and it's essential we don't over expose it.' A coordinator is engaged to look after weddings, but Kate and Simon take on most of the other events, including visits by various clubs, and outdoor luncheons for groups. Recently Kate took a film producer on a familiarisation tour, opening up possibilities. Maybe an Australian version of *Downton Abbey*?

The Tol's are fast learning that some types of events take more work than others. 'We just get in casual help when we need it,' says Kate. For the privileged few wanting to stay longer and soak up the magic of Mount Mitchell, there is an historic cottage and brick-veneer family home available for casual hire. Kate continues to manage their Moonambel property, which is also available for luxury Australian bush experiences.

It becomes evident during our conversation that the Tol's are good at connecting with the right people and that those relationships are helping to strengthen their vision for Mount Mitchell. In the initial stages they employed Kate Davis, an events coordinator. She helped establish the brand. Each discussion leads to someone else. 'Everyone gets as passionate about Mount Mitchell as we are,' says Kate. 'It's just such a special place. There are moments I love, every day. We are constantly pinching ourselves!'

Kate continues to access workshops and courses as time permits, continually building her skills and exploring new ideas, as they seek that sweet spot between business and lifestyle. Marketing through the Pyrenees Tourism Board, Visit Ballarat, and word-of-mouth referrals are proving most effective.

One gets the impression that Kate and Simon have spent their lives gathering the appropriate knowledge and complementary skills required to make Mount Mitchell a viable business. And they aren't afraid to take on something new. Following their instincts may not be a risk after all.

'Always challenged, rarely defeated,' quips Simon, who acknowledges 2020 has been difficult at times. They survived a couple of bushfire scares thanks to the quick support of their neighbours, and can only host weddings and events at the property when coronavirus restrictions aren't in force.

'We've laid low the past year,' Kate admits. 'While we do enjoy sharing the garden with visiting groups, we don't want to get too commercial. This is our home and we're very settled now. The house just seems to love us. I think it needed children, noise, parties and skateboards!'

In their most exciting news, the Waubra Football Club won the 2019 Premiership under Simon's presidency. 'We can call ourselves locals now,' she laughs. 'There is no way I'd go back, to my previous life!' agrees Simon.

SIMON & KATE'S BUSINESS TIPS:

- Just do it and have fun.
- Take sensible risks.
- Get involved and give back to your local community.

www.mountmitchell.com.au

Retro Respection

Storm Hurst and Joleen Brown, Retro Respection

Not many businesses can claim to have been instigated by a triple cake-stacking canister, but this happens to be the case when it comes to Retro Respection, a quirky homeware, giftware and vintage lovers' shop in Collie, Western Australia. Its two equally quirky business partners are an inspiration to all those young mums who may feel trapped at home.

With the newly opened Retro Respection store creating a buzz in Collie, I popped in to catch up with its two enterprising business partners, Storm Hurst and Joleen Brown. As young mums, it was rare for both of them to be in the store at the same time. Straightaway it became evident that they are passionate about their products, in the way they dress and what they stock in the store, sometimes purely for conversational purposes.

It also proved to be my most challenging and fun interview of 2018. Challenging because they tend to bounce off each other like rubber balls when it comes to conversation, and fun because of their determination to enjoy life to its fullest.

Yes, it is true that a triple cake-stacking canister caught Storm's attention at playgroup way back in 2012. 'A mother asked if anyone wanted one and I said, 'I'll have that!'' recalls Storm. In the early days of her business she sold vintage items on eBay as a hobby.

Joleen is another local young mother interested in vintage goods and writing a blog – they laugh as they recall a particularly hideous tea set she had collected. She soon caught Storm's attention. 'We had kids the same age and just hit it off,' says Joleen. 'And I had the blog,' she adds knowingly.

'Joleen kept buying stuff at garage sales putting us in direct competition, so it made sense for us to team up,' explains Storm, pointedly ignoring the blog reference. 'I love the history and do the research.'

'Whereas I just jump in with random ideas,' says Joleen.

'Yes, Joleen likes to try new things,' confirms Storm, 'whereas I think things through. She relies on me to pull her back in. We make a great team.'

'We never expected it to be an overnight success,' admits Joleen.

'We're brought up to think we can do anything but once you have kids the reality is that you don't leave the house,' says Storm. 'This business has been built around family. We have set it up so we are always available for our kids.'

In 2012 Storm started selling online from her family home in Collie. Stock took up lots of space. When she joined forces with Joleen in 2014 they came up with the quirky name Retro Respection. 'It's a wicked name,' Joleen grins.

'An important lesson when starting the business was to leverage our circumstances,' recalls Storm. 'As a mum without a paid job, I couldn't even get a credit card!' Fortunately, a supportive aunt lent her money to get started and has been one of her biggest fans.

Storm and Joleen have chosen to work without wages, pouring their earnings back into the business, which originally focused on sales through eBay, and now through their own website.

In September 2018 they took the unusual step of expanding their online business to a shopfront in their hometown of Collie. A six-month trial of a vacant shop at a reduced rent suited their tight budget. In a brave step they opened seven days a week, one of very few businesses to do so in this working town, but perhaps a forerunner to positive change.

Their calculated gamble paid off. With increased visibility and an expanded range of stock, sales immediately increased. 'It's been good for the locals,' confirms Storm. 'Sometimes people just come in for a chat and now visitors passing through town on weekends drop in to browse.'

'Our reputation is everything and we've been professional right from the beginning,' says Storm. (Or maybe it was Joleen? My head is spinning with these two dynamos!) 'No shortcuts!' This was agreed unanimously.

Without a budget for marketing they have relied on organic growth through Facebook and Instagram and paid careful attention to the statistics. 'Every time we post SALE it goes crazy,' Joleen adds with a smile.

Opening their shopfront made a point-of-sale system a priority. After much trial and error they settled on Neto, which provides a basic do-it-yourself website template and, most importantly, synchronises their inventory and sales in the shop, and across the website and eBay platforms. 'Once you learn a new system you get better each time, and more adaptable,' says Storm.

On the few occasions they are in the same room, this dynamic duo spends time strategically planning their new lines. With a strong following of online collectors, brooches were quite successful when introduced. 'Consumables such as lollies and dog treats also invite repeat buyers,' says Storm. 'And we'd love to get more sustainable products in.'

'While we haven't made serious money yet, we enjoy what we're doing,' says Storm. 'Joleen and I are best buddies and each other's biggest supporters.'

'We're taking it day by day and enjoying ourselves,' Joleen confirms.

At the end of a whirlwind interview, Storm announces that this is only the start of their grand plan. 'We're going to bed down this shop and make it a destination; refine the website, expand the shop space, expand the product lines, and maybe open a whole bunch of shops.'

I came away thinking that they just might do that but then the COVID-19 restrictions were introduced in March 2020. Their physical shopfront temporarily closed but their already established online sales platform gave them a strong advantage.

'Yes, we shut the doors for a month with children at home,' Storm confirms. 'Online sales and a few phone orders have enabled us to survive. We've noticed older people suddenly realising that online shopping isn't all that bad.'

In response to community needs they increased their hand sanitiser and soap ranges. The 'I'm stuck at home with you bastards' hygienic range particularly caught my eye.

Joleen, the extrovert, has been busy doing Facebook live chats about gift ideas and introducing their new in-house range of pet treats and resident expert. Free home deliveries were promoted to locals.

'We've always dropped things off to locals at no charge but just advertised it more during the restrictions,' explains Storm. 'It is going to be interesting to see what happens over the next year, but I think we are well positioned to keep doing well. Things are improving again and we will keep working on consolidating our financial position.'

These two may not have achieved their tongue-in-cheek vision of opening a chain of stores yet, but they have moved to a new storefront in the same street to accommodate an increase in stock, and they are still having a lot of fun.

STORM & JOLEEN'S TOP BUSINESS TIPS:

- Be passionate about your products.
- Be stubborn.
- Don't be afraid to take that leap.
- Be a nimble bull.

www.retrorespection.com.au

Passionate

When you love what you do the hours just fly by and even mundane tasks are willingly undertaken with a smile on your face, because you understand they are necessary to help achieve your goal. Those who can match a hobby or an interest with a business are truly flying high. It could simply be putting your strengths into action. Maybe it is the satisfaction of being your own boss, or you love meeting customer needs and solving their problems. Perhaps you love the challenge of doing what others said couldn't be done! There are many factors that contribute to success in business, but it is truly a bonus when you can do what you love.

Looking back on the business stories I've shared over the years, 'passionate' is a word I've often used to describe the business owners interviewed.

'It's easy to train people who already have a passion.'

A fascination with wild camels enticed Chris and Megan Williams to establish the Camel Milk Co. Australia and they have found it to be a drawcard for employees who share their passion.

'I am a hot rodder. We talk the same language and have the same interests.'

Likewise, Larry O'Toole was obsessed with street rodding and became publisher of *Australian Street Rodding*, a magazine that has survived and thrived where many have failed.

'We're family owned, and we're involved in the whole process from planting, to the pruning and training of the vines, as well as the picking and packaging of the end product.'

While most kids went to playgroup and kindergarten, Katerina and Ivana Blekic grew up working alongside their parents in the family vineyard near

Mildura. Today, they are busy establishing the building blocks of their own business enterprise, The Sultana Sisters.

'We have these incredible forestry tracks around Collie and mountain biking is a huge growth area.'

In Western Australia Erik Mellegers turned his cycling hobby into a business that is now creating opportunities for his traditional coal-mining community.

'It (the building) could have been leased to any number of people but it seemed right to give these two young guys the opportunity.'

Back in Central Victoria, Edward and Dale followed their passion for sport into the fitness industry. A game-changing conversation with a local businessman gave them a head start on their journey into business.

As their stories demonstrate, if you have a passion for your business it helps make those mundane tasks and tough days bearable, and the good days an absolute joy.

Camel Milk Co Australia

Chris and Megan Williams, Camel Milk Co Australia

Chris and Megan Williams of Camel Milk Co Australia believed 2018 would be the Year of the Camel. While there has been no official proclamation, indications are that their Kyabram-based business will be worthy of such accolades.

With traditional dairy businesses under pressure it is no surprise that rural communities are rapidly diversifying, becoming home to a wider range of micro businesses. But camels? Seriously? Two questions immediately sprang to mind. How on earth do you milk a camel? And why on earth would you want to?

A road trip on a hot January morning in 2018 helped me answer these two questions. The first question was easily resolved by arriving right on milking time to see the mobile milking units operating alongside a race. Which brings us to the why.

We managed to wrangle Chris off a tractor to sit down with Megan so I could hear their fascinating story firsthand, delivered in half sentences that they finish for each other, a charming testimony to a shared passion. And, to their secret delight, I request milk when offered a coffee.

From modest beginnings in 2014 with three camels on 40 hectares, Chris and Megan have expanded their business to nearly 250 camels on 200 hectares with plans for further expansion. Straightaway this indicates what a success story it has been but not without the usual risk and hard work associated with a start-up business.

Working with Megan's parents on their Victorian dairy farm, the newly married couple were looking for something agriculture based, but different. While researching what they could do, their family expanded with the arrival of three active boys in less than four years.

'We were looking at getting our own farm and getting the work–life balance going,' says Chris. 'It was important to have a sustainable income and avoid having all our eggs in the one basket.' They looked at miniature Herefords and goats before settling on camels.

To understand why camels were their beast of choice we must back pedal to when they met in 2008. Chris had just emigrated from the United Kingdom to work on a cattle station east of Alice Springs. Megan was driving tourist coaches. They met in a pub in Alice Springs, as you do.

In what appears to be love at first sight, Megan jumped ship – or coach to be accurate – and started working with Chris on Andado Station, where camels roam wild. They became fascinated with these majestic animals, imported in the 19th century to help build the telegraph from Adelaide to

Darwin and eventually abandoned to roam free and breed to feral numbers.

When the couple moved to Megan's family property in Victoria, where drought, rising expenses and declining income has seen the water-dependent dairy industry struggle, they brought with them the knowledge that camels survive well in the harshest of climates. But surely milking camels was unheard of in Victoria?

'Dad always says that if you are a farmer you are one of the biggest gamblers in the world,' laughs Megan. 'We didn't know for sure if there was a market,' she acknowledges but, incredibly, as soon as word got out there was a waiting list – and they hadn't even started producing milk.

What started out as Camel Milk Victoria was soon rebranded Camel Milk Co Australia when it turned out that fresh camel's milk is highly sought by a large Middle Eastern customer base in Melbourne, Sydney and Perth, through fine grocers and boutique stalls.

'In their countries camel milk is a staple,' says Megan. 'Australia has a huge advantage over other countries because we have disease-free camels. Once you have a recognised brand in Australia, then it is trusted overseas as well.' As a result, they are already exporting milk to Hong Kong and Singapore and supplies are about to hit Iran. A shortage in the United States is another opportunity they are currently pursuing.

With high protein and low fat, camel's milk is also attractive to the fitness market. It doesn't even occur to me that I'm drinking camel's milk in my coffee until pointed out by Megan. My initial thought is that it tastes similar to skim milk.

Having resolved the 'How?' and 'Why?' we turn to the many challenges of starting a new business enterprise, not to mention such an unusual one. Their initial pilot with three camels proved they were on to a solid business idea. It was time to purchase more land and more camels. 'Your bank would be more than willing to help?' I ask the question tongue in cheek and inevitably Megan fires up. 'You see bank adverts that encourage you to do something new, niche and innovative but it's a load of crock! We changed banks and it was positive for a while, but the final decision was made by people in the city who have no idea.' Instead, the sale of some dairy heifers helped them get started.

Not relying on finance and taking a staged approach turned out to be a huge positive. 'We had to make the money before we could spend it,' explains Chris. 'The advantage is that we own everything,' adds Megan. 'It's good to grow into business, not go into business.'

Sourcing camels has also been tricky. 'It's not as easy as buying dairy heifers,' Chris admits. Usually they are mustered directly from the outback. Their request for pregnant female camels hasn't always been adhered to resulting in one load that included bulls and calves being sent back. When possible they now go and help draft the camels after mustering.

With a fourteen-month gestation, trying to guess the stage of the pregnancy is another constant challenge. Now they have their own bulls and breeding program this is becoming easier. Feed issues were overcome by finding a 'fantastic' nutritionist who helped them formulate their diet.

The fact that the majority of camels are wild or semi wild is a significant challenge that requires dedicated and skilled staff. When the couple first advertised for an experienced camel milker it was met with much laughter, but social media and word of mouth got results.

'First they have to have an absolute love of camels and skills from being around camels,' explains Megan. 'It's easy to train people who already have a passion.' As a result, they have a multicultural workforce with the majority of their seven staff members having either lived or travelled in countries that have camels. When it is time for them to move on, they are often able to recommend someone to take their place.

Chris and Megan willingly undertook to meet the stringent Australian food production and handling regulations, including installation of a pasteuriser plant and cool room. Both have an Advanced Diploma in Agriculture, which has helped them along the way, but doing their own research and connecting with the right people in the industry has been crucial to their success. Attending trade fairs has also been a productive investment.

Finding an independent niche distributor took some time and was aided by the many connections formed at a Naturally Good Expo in Sydney. 'We did it ourselves at first,' says Chris. 'Started with a Wayco in the back of the car then upgraded to a refrigerated vehicle.' They now enjoy a friendly twice-weekly pick up by Melbourne-based Metro Milk, which simultaneously provides a service to many other small producers in rural Victoria.

Once the business expanded into an international market, it became evident that their customers like a range, not just one product. In addition to fresh camel's milk, they now also sell soaps, lip balms, body butters, liquid soaps and powdered milk. Research and development continue with a current focus on introducing camel cheese and chocolate products, no mean feat with up to six months required to get to point of sale.

'We have a lot of money tied up in this, which we can only hope to get back,' Chris admits.

'Yes, it's a bit of a gamble,' Megan agrees, 'particularly ensuring that we have enough milk to meet demand. We have to meet all the regulations, produce samples, test the market, get customer feedback, and design packaging before we can even start selling.' Outsourcing some aspects of the business was a wise decision made early on. A professional is contracted to look after their website and the non-fresh products are packaged offsite.

Despite all the challenges of setting up and continuing to grow Camel Milk Co Australia, Chris and Megan have no doubt they are on the right track. 'It's very exciting being our own bosses and doing something different,' admits Megan. 'We're constantly learning,' agrees Chris, 'and we're making a living from something we've made from scratch. There's money in everything if you do it properly.'

Putting back into the community is something else they enjoy. 'Employing people and bringing them to live in Kyabram probably gives the pub a lot of business,' Chris smiles. 'We also bring visitors to town, give tours of the farm and point out other nearby attractions,' Megan adds. A feature on ABC's *Landline* program is giving them and the district added exposure. 'We all need to understand the ramifications of what happens to rural towns when local agriculture isn't supported,' says Megan.

Being able to have their young boys close at hand has been a priority. While a nanny comes in daily to allow them both to work in the business, the boys often join them when feeding the camels and they always eat meals together.

'We want them to grow up and have opportunities. Already they are learning lots of skills as a normal part of their life,' says Chris.

Fast-forward to 2020 and Megan and Chris have been busy welcoming new distributors of their products. They can mostly be found in major centres including Melbourne, Sydney, South Australia and Singapore. 'Thailand has just come on board as well,' Megan is pleased to advise.

'We've had an absolutely, massive boom in camel milk powder sales, which has in turn supported the sale of our skin-care range, especially online. There has been a huge increase from the Asian market.'

As part of their breeding program they are continuing to grow the number of camels on the farm. 'We have well over 300 camels now.'

Camel Milk Co Australia has been working with Melbourne University on camel milk and health benefits and Megan is looking forward to sharing the outcomes. Their farm shop is a popular spot for locals to purchase goods. When coronavirus restrictions are not in place, tours are also welcomed provided they are booked.

'Tours give an opportunity to look, see and touch what we do here, a real glimpse into our day-to-day work,' Megan smiles.

I ask about the children. 'Two at school and one at kinder. I don't know about work–life balance, I think a mum's work life is just to get to the end of the day!'

CHRIS & MEGAN'S TOP BUSINESS TIPS:

- Do your research.
- Be passionate about what you are doing.
- Educate yourself on what you are going to do.
- Don't doubt yourself.
- Be a problem solver.

www.camelmilkco.com.au

Graffiti Publications

Larry O'Toole, Graffiti Publications

How often do we hear that we should do what we love? In 2017, Graffiti Publications and its flagship magazine Australian Street Rodding *celebrated 40 years of achievement. Larry O'Toole has not only survived but thrived in this cutthroat industry, while many other specialist publishers have come and gone.*

Chatting with a semi-retired Larry in his Castlemaine-based business that employs six people, it becomes clear that there are two key factors to the business's longevity: being authentic and customer focused pretty much sums it up.

Ask him what the magazine is about, and Larry has no hesitation in responding. 'Owning, building and modifying street vehicles with an emphasis on pre 1948.' In addition, Graffiti Publications prints and franchises over 300 specialist books and DVDs relating to the modified car industry. 'We know our audience, which is why the big corporates fail,' explains Larry. 'I am a hot rodder. We talk the same language and have the same interests.'

Growing up on the family farm near Swan Hill, Larry learned driving and mechanical skills at an early age. His interest in street rodding was sparked as a teenager. 'One day I picked up a hot rod magazine and instantly knew what I wanted to do.'

Ever since there has been a project in progress in Larry's back shed; an interest that brought him to Central Victoria in 1973. He was part of the first wave of street rodding enthusiasts drawn to Castlemaine, where interesting things were happening in this field. Many of these enthusiasts started out with backyard hobbies and, like Graffiti Publications, evolved into successful businesses.

Four partners formed Graffiti Publications in 1976 as an after-hours enterprise. With a disappointingly slow start and personal circumstances intervening, three of the partners sold their shares to Larry and wife Mary, who became the sole owners in 1989.

Mary has worked hard to provide administrative support in between raising their four children, and their son Allister now handles the bulk of the editorial production work, but Larry is undoubtedly still the public face of the business. Over the past 40 years he has attended all the major events across Australia to chat with enthusiasts and gather knowledge and material for the magazine. In addition, he has attended the American Street Rod Nationals for over 30 years.

With such diligent research Larry knows his market well. Rather than being driven by advertising, Graffiti Publications is unashamedly customer focused, creating a loyal subscription base Australia wide that is critical for success. Attention is paid to rewarding members of the Graffiti Club with special offers and a free advertisement to sell their cars. A newsletter promotes inside and breaking news. 'It's a bit more work but the return is good,' says Larry.

'If you produce good content you don't have to ram advertising down the readers' throats,' says Larry. 'We only include advertising that is beneficial to our readers as well as to the advertiser.'

I can see, flicking through the latest edition, how the magazine promotes a sense of community with its reports from clubs and events across Australia and New Zealand.

Sharing knowledge is another important component of the magazine. 'Readers appreciate the learning element of our magazine and love watching projects take shape in instalments in backyard sheds. We have six columnists sharing their technical expertise each month.'

Among other skills, Larry excels at planning and timing. Graffiti has never missed a publishing date, crucial in an industry where being one day late can push a print run back a week.

In addition to the mechanical skills learnt on the farm, Larry pays credit to a brief career in photography and pre-production with the *Swan Hill Guardian* that provided him with a valuable overview of the publishing industry. The rest of his operating skills have been developed along the way and by attending tradeshows and business development events. 'I'm always learning,' he admits, 'but most often I learn from others how *not* to do it!'

Whiteboards enable staff to plan day-to-day operations, and the publication schedule is set up to 12 months ahead to stay on top of multiple deadlines. In-house production right up until the print-ready phase helps control both quality and timing to minimise delays.

'Our customers are die-hard enthusiasts and expect their magazine to be delivered at the same time each month. Unfortunately, Australia Post is creating a challenge for us. What used to take two to three days is now taking in excess of a week,' he admits with a hint of frustration.

Larry's planning skills also benefit the industry and wider community. Looking decidedly weary, he has just participated in Graffiti's 40th anniversary celebrations and the Boogaloo Invitational held at Castlemaine and coinciding with the largest ever Australian Street Rod Nationals held in nearby Bendigo. All this was perfectly timed to entice over a thousand enthusiasts to the region for the entire month and entertain huge numbers of spectators.

Timing is king. A full-colour catalogue printed in October, just prior to Christmas each year, promotes Graffiti's offerings including specialist books and DVDs. 'It works like magic,' says Larry.

At a time when everyone is embracing the digital era, Larry is bluntly dismissive of online publications. 'Too many have gone down that path and failed.' Graffiti has a website to sell its products and utilises social media to complement their marketing, but that is as far as it goes. A discerning businessman, he instead identifies opportunities such as acting as a franchise for overseas specialist publications popular in Australia. A sister magazine, *Hot Rodding International*, is currently being positioned to take on the global market utilising new distribution techniques.

Improving technologies have clearly impacted on production and printing over the past 40 years. There is an impressive collection of past computers, film processors and typesetters used throughout the magazine's history but Larry is quick to caution against being an early adopter. 'Don't rush into new technology,' he advises. 'Let them iron out all the bugs first. But stay informed on emerging technology so you know when to make the move.'

When I catch up with Larry again in 2020 he reiterates: 'Print is still valid and wanted by customers. There was a backlash by customers in the United States when a corporate publisher recently slashed a number of its printed publications because it pursued online publication as a priority. Specialised publications like ours aren't threatened by online publications, but our customers can be distracted in a digital world. We have to work hard to keep their attention.

'The biggest danger,' he adds, 'is from the service industries that surround our printed publications. They are in danger of failing, putting our distribution and delivery under pressure. It's frustrating and can hurt our type of business and is often outside our control.'

Graffiti Publications has kept busy during the coronavirus restrictions. 'COVID has only reinforced my original perception with an increase in subscriptions and strong sales though our website,' says Larry. 'People were looking for something that interests them while in lock-down.'

Sure and steady with an authentic customer focus, there is no doubt that *Australian Street Rodding* is Australia's longest running magazine in this genre for a very good reason. I have no doubt they are well on track for their 50th anniversary celebrations in 2027.

LARRY'S TOP BUSINESS TIPS:

- Be customer focused.
- Reward your loyal customers.
- Plan well ahead.
- Control your own processes as much as you can.
- Don't rush into new technology, let them iron the bugs out first.

  www.graffitipub.com.au

The Sultana Sisters

Katerina and Ivana Blekic, The Sultana Sisters
(Courtesy *Sunraysia Daily*, Mildura)

Armed with university degrees, Mildura sisters Katerina and Ivana Blekic are employed for the first time in their lives away from the family's vineyard. However, far from turning their back on agriculture, they are spending every spare minute working on their new business enterprise, The Sultana Sisters. In an industry dominated by large international companies they have carefully crafted their brand to attract a local and online market.

When John Blekic, a migrant from Croatia, planted his first vines on the outskirts of Mildura in the late 1950s, he would never have guessed that 60 years later his two granddaughters would be branding themselves as The Sultana Sisters. While most kids went to playgroup and kindergarten, Katerina and Ivana grew up working alongside their parents in the family vineyard. By 2018, aged 22 and 24, they were busy establishing the building blocks of their own business enterprise. With picking almost completed, their next exciting step was to pack and launch their brand.

I caught up with Katerina and Ivana on Good Friday, one of the few days of the year the family downs tools. With half of this year's family crop sitting in the sheds, they were praying for no rain (it darkens the fruit) and anticipated that by Easter Monday they would have the second half picked. A small portion of this year's family crop had been allocated to The Sultana Sisters, about to launch their new Australian brand in an increasingly global market. 'We have a big vision,' says Katerina, 'but we're starting off small and seeing where it goes.'

They officially formed the business in March 2017, giving away samples to test the market. 'We are taking the time to get to know our market and ourselves as a brand,' Ivana confirms. Not happy with their initial branding as Mallee Dried Fruits they invested in a graphic designer who understood their vision and are excitedly waiting for the new packaging to arrive. 'It's unique packaging, printed with a bright colour on craft paper with plastic lining and a clear window to display the product,' Ivana explains. 'We want it to come across as vibrant and fun.'

They are very clear on their need to differentiate in a global market and also understand that it won't happen overnight. 'Mildura produces a large quantity of Australia's dried fruits and is home to many large corporations,' says Katerina. 'By comparison we're a small fish in a big sea so we want to be different. We're family owned, and we're involved in the whole process from the planting, to the pruning and training of the vines, as well as the picking and packaging of the product.'

'We're aiming to provide a fresh look to the market,' says Ivana. 'And we're big planners,' adds Katerina. 'We want to do this right.' Katerina set up a website using a Squarespace template in preparation for online sales, her high social media presence giving them a head start with the marketing. Ivana takes responsibility for the accounting side of the business utilising her accounting and legal skills.

These young women are high achievers. Upon completing her degree in Community and Sustainable Development, Katerina was offered a place in the Ruralco Graduate Program. Passionate about social justice, Ivana is putting her law and accounting degree to good use as a tenant advocate for Haven Home Safe covering the region from Mildura to Kerang. During 2017 Katerina was both a National Rural Ambassador finalist for the Agriculture Show and a Leo (youth) Lion giving her access to state and nationwide networks. Her photographs on Instagram and Facebook taken among the vines and machinery are attracting interest. 'I am documenting a day in the life of what we do in the vineyard,' Katerina explains. Bridging the divide between consumers and farmers is a personal quest for both sisters. They dream of one day producing a book featuring The Sultana Sisters, a way of reaching young people and sharing their passion for agriculture.

Katerina and Ivana completed their degrees by correspondence, allowing them to continue working full time in the family vineyards while studying. Working away from the farm for the first time in 2018 gave them a better perspective of the markets they intend to reach through their new business.

On weekends, and sometimes even before and after their paid work, the sisters are busy out in the vineyard and working on their business. They explain the different techniques for naturally dried sultanas on the vine (which are dark in colour) as opposed to the golden sultanas that are put through a wetting machine and sprayed with potash and oil to get their unique colour. Even though the change from flood to drip irrigation took place 18 years ago when both were toddlers, they also talk about what a significant improvement this has been, a reminder they have grown up in the industry.

A more recent project involves converting a building into a new operation centre and office. They plan to use the top level leaving the ground floor for their parents and a storefront. 'I love working in spaces that are bright and creative,' Katerina says.

They have established a cashless system in preparation for the launch of their product at farmers' markets around the region. 'We're keen on Apple products,' says Katerina, 'and decided on the Square range of devices that plug into your iPhone and provide point of sale software.'

Bakeries and health food and corner stores are potential customers in addition to direct sales. 'While investors and super farms exist in the region, we want to show that smaller growers can be sustainable if they deal direct,' says Katerina.

With the benefit of growing up in the family vineyard and their individual skills and networks, these enterprising sisters are building on the strong foundations set in place by Grandpa Blekic and their parents, adding their own unique building blocks to the Sunraysia business landscape. The Sultana Sisters successfully launched two core products on the market in late 2018. In 2020 their sales are gathering momentum and Katerina reports that demand sees them almost out of product.

'Our main customers have been bakeries, cafes and specialty stores but we aim to expand our customer base past our region. We have been contacted multiple times for export but don't have the capacity at the moment,' says Katerina.

With their passion for agricultural shows, the girls signed up in 2019 for three years as naming rights sponsors in the Victorian Agricultural Shows Ltd fruit cake competition categories. 'This year we are planning to launch our blog Sultana Sunday, giving consumers an insight into The Sultana Sisters, the industry, and how produce is grown.'

During the coronavirus restrictions they have been working on their idea for a children's book.

Clearly Katerina and Ivana know how to reach their target audiences and it helps that everyone loves to support young people in business.

Crank'n Cycles

Erik Mellegers, Crank'n Cycles

'Sometimes doors open; as is meant to happen', observes Erik Mellegers, from the doorway of his business Crank'n Cycles in the town of Collie, Western Australia. In 2017, approaching his 11th year in business, he reflected on where it all began. As is often the case, it started with a hobby.

Erik spent his early years in Holland surrounded by bicycles, but it wasn't until his family emigrated to Australia that cycling became a passion. A charismatic teacher at Erik's high school in Collie set the wheels in motion when he introduced cycling as a sport. Even then, it wasn't until the family moved from Collie to Australind some years later that he took the next step.

While in Year 10 Erik had, like many his age, a part-time job at a local supermarket. He rode his racing bike to and from work, a 32-kilometre round trip, and was encouraged by a co-worker to enter local cycling events. Erik had always enjoyed his riding but had never raced; he didn't think he'd be good enough to compete. Eventually persuaded he turned up at a road time trial with the Bunbury Cycling Club. His childhood hero (a high school teacher and the record holder of the event) was there. Erik raced, and to his surprise defeated his former teacher by four seconds to win the event. He realised he was actually pretty good at racing, and it concreted his lifelong love for cycling.

Following a short stint at university, and deciding that engineering wasn't for him, he determined he wanted to own a bike shop – even if it was for the sake of just hanging out with likeminded people and supplying his own sporting needs. 'But I couldn't get the money together,' recalls Erik when a Bunbury cycle shop came up for sale. 'I was a struggling and broke twenty-year-old.'

Instead Erik embarked on a retail career with Retravision and Harvey Norman, working his way into management positions and learning valuable customer service, stock inventory, and financial skills along the way. 'The retail training was awesome, and I found myself getting sucked into the corporate franchise world, meeting targets, and working towards owning my own franchise store. Then I saw the bad side of franchising and decided it wasn't for me.'

That decision allowed Erik to return to his love of cycling and he applied to work as a salesman at a Bunbury-based cycle shop. 'It was a huge pay cut, but I put it to the owners that potentially I could buy into the business in the future.'

Erik's plan faltered when the business came up for sale within 18 months; he still wasn't in a good enough financial position to buy in. It was gut-wrenching when the business was sold to another buyer. But fate decided to smile on him in another way. Within six months Western Australia's housing boom increased his home equity giving him some buying power. He decided to take a road trip back to his childhood hometown of Collie.

'I remember driving up Roelands Hill and thinking I can't believe I'm driving to Collie,' Erik smiles in recollection. Bikes R Us, the local cycle and toyshop, had been on the market for a couple of years. 'I walked into the shop, saw the potential and bit the bullet,' says Erik. A business loan was quickly secured with his home as collateral. A career in retail had prepared Erik for this moment. 'I opened accounts and bought a heap of stock before I was handed the keys to the shop. Through Harvey Norman I'd learnt how to retail, I had the supplier contacts from my work with the cycling shop, and I knew consumers.'

Of course, it wasn't all smooth sailing. Erik still recalls the painful aftermath of his first Christmas in business. 'I sold heaps of stuff up until Christmas and kept ordering in new stock.' By the end of January, traditionally a quiet time for retailers, he found himself looking at a huge pile of outstanding bills. Rather than curl up into the foetal position, Erik decided to just 'roll with it'. He explained the situation to his suppliers and negotiated paying off the bills over an extended period of time. I have heard this referred to as the 'third bank' in business circles, and the reason why everyone should have a good relationship and open communication with their suppliers. Erik has always attended supplier events and shown a genuine interest in their products.

Despite their understanding of the situation, there was still an important lesson learnt. 'I had to learn to manage what level of stock I could get away with' – although he admits to still stocking the 'cool' stuff ranging from top-of-the-line road-racing bicycles to the fat-tyred mountain bikes. And everything in between.

I realise that Erik is a man who notes his milestones. Winning the cycle race and deciding he wanted to own a cycle shop was one. Ask him how long he has been in business and he immediately answers, 'Since 18 February 2007.' The third milestone is a significant one for a young man who has created an income to support a simple lifestyle. 'Getting married and having a child forced me to go from living in the back of the shop and running it as a hobby to running it as a business and making money.'

Even as a small business owner with part-time support staff, Erik has deliberately kept the processes simple with no elaborate stock-tracking systems. 'I don't spend money unnecessarily,' he admits, 'but this would have to change if I ever employ a manager.'

Erik continues to generously stock the shop with a diverse range of cycles to create a welcoming and stimulating destination for cyclists of all genres, but he is aware of which lines turn over more quickly and which offer the biggest profit margins. A children's toy section offers sales diversity. The original shop was expanded into next door when it came up for lease.

Erik is excited about the future of the Collie region. In 2017 he helped to lead community conversations as part of the Operation Next Gen program. In late 2018 the Western Australian Government announced $10 million funding to develop mountain bike riding trails through the Collie region, something Erik has worked hard to achieve. By 2020 the plans are coming to fruition.

'I've been working in the background for 15 years ready for Collie to turn into a trail town and the advocacy is finally paying off. I'm still chair of the Collie Mountain Bike Club but I'm learning to say no to other things,' Erik confides. 'It's great that people are now getting paid to do what I was part of starting so I can sit back a bit more.' While he has been excited about developing a new trail hub business proposal, until sufficient investment becomes available Erik has taken a break to remain focused on his retail business.

With a slow economy the past few years he has concentrated on reducing overheads to remain competitive. 'We've shrunk the shop space down by one rental but have just as much stock crammed into a smaller space. Because we've established such a good reputation, we've also been able to reduce advertising costs.'

'During the coronavirus restrictions in 2020, we lost a lot of out-of-town sales when people couldn't travel, but still sold more bikes locally than we have for the last couple of years for the same period. So, good for us! Now stock availability is becoming an issue though. We do carry quite a bit of stock, so it should tide us over the worst of the stock shortage issues.'

Wanting to spend more time with his young family, Erik has employed another full-time staff member.

Definitely no longer a hobby!

ERIK'S TOP BUSINESS TIPS:

- Know what you are getting yourself into. Do your research and get experience by working for others first.
- Ensure you have a strong support group. Sit down with your family and make sure they are on board.
- Build a good community network if starting a business in a new area, i.e. Rotary Club, sporting groups.
- Don't get into business if you're a worrier. It can be rocky but you have to look at the long-term benefits.
- Take time out for yourself.

  www.crankncycles.com.au

Maine Fitness

Edward Coulthard and Dale Hansford, Maine Fitness

Celebrating the first year of a new business in 2016 was a major milestone for 23-year-old Edward Coulthard and 24-year-old Dale Hansford, co-owners of Maine Fitness located in a newly refurbished industrial shed in Castlemaine, Central Victoria. By 2020 Edward has a new partner, exciting plans, and a huge challenge with COVID-19.

Touring their new business premises in 2016, the spacious facility had a professional feel and, even to my uneducated eye, the equipment looked high quality. It was no surprise when Dale described the business as 'a high-class professional gymnasium' for those over 16 years of age.

While one of their 220 current members is doing impressive chin pull-ups on a bar across the room, my brain is doing mental gymnastics and I'm bursting to ask the question. How on earth were these two young men able to afford the start-up investment in a quality venue and equipment, not to mention the marketing needed to grow a membership?

It appears that this enterprising pair has invested significant time but minimal capital into approaching and building the business in a smart way to make it affordable and successful, in an industry they are passionate about.

Back in late 2014, the concept of Maine Fitness moved into overdrive when the local newspaper featured an article on Glenn Guest, a local businessman and property owner. Glenn was publicly announcing his intention to refurbish one of his properties, an industrial shed, as a modern gymnasium. Edward was devastated. This was his vision and he had been working hard and saving to see it come to fruition. He and Dale had just started to scope out another potential site for a gymnasium. With both young men growing up and playing sport together in Castlemaine, and having worked in Melbourne in the personal training industry, it was a logical decision to pool their expertise and capital enabling them to live and work in their home town as business partners.

After reading Glenn's announcement in the local newspaper, it seemed their plans needed to be revised. 'I knew it would be difficult to compete with a gym of this size,' says Edward. That was until a game-changing conversation took place. Edward's football coach approached Glenn on their behalf, and it turned out he was open to proposals.

As Glenn explains: 'After being leased short term, our building was in danger of sitting empty and I was simply looking for a long-term financial return. Castlemaine lacked a quality gymnasium and it was the ideal opportunity for this space, so I made the commitment to refurbish it for this purpose. It was never my intention to be there full time because of my other business interests.'

With the opportunity to fast track their business idea, Edward and Dale quickly put a proposal together. 'Looking at what other successful businesses in the industry were doing was our starting point,' explains Dale. 'Then we took educated guesses as to how the business would progress, being as conservative as we could be but still playing the odds.'

'Edward and Dale had some good ideas and the experience to run a gymnasium to the standard I wanted,' Glenn recalls. 'We'd invested a lot of money in fitting out the building and wanted it to be inviting for all ages. It could have been leased to any number of people, but it seemed right to give these two young guys the opportunity.' Maine Fitness was suddenly in take-off mode!

Glenn Guest, Maine Fitness landlord

Having secured the perfect venue, the next challenge was to fit it out with quality gymnasium equipment. 'Once again, leasing was the best option for us,' says Dale. With a tight three-month schedule the two new business partners and their landlord threw themselves into ensuring the facility was ready for opening day. Family and friends happily helped by assembling the equipment in the final few weeks. 'It was crazy,' Edwards grins.

With opening day approaching and funds flowing out of their limited bank account, they came up with another great idea. 'One really smart thing we did,' Dale says, 'was sell memberships before the gym opened. Sharing photos of the facilities with details of our qualifications and offering a discounted membership got us over 20 members and created cash flow in advance.'

Facebook has proven to be the most cost-effective promoter of the business. Now they are operational, word-of-mouth recommendations are equally powerful and their membership has grown to 220 in just 12 months.

In early 2016 the Victorian Drug Free Power Lifting Association conducted a novice event at Maine Fitness citing it as one of the most successful they had held with 20 participants and over 100 spectators. Following this success, the Central Victorian Power Lifting Championships were also held there with sponsorship from another local business, Centre State Drilling, to support a local lifting team to participate.

Edward and Dale work full-time in a business open seven days a week, sharing duties with three employees. With the high-energy levels I can only vaguely recall from my youth, they are working long hours. They also invest in updating their skills by attending courses all over Australia.

While satisfied with the results so far, Dale admits he is looking forward to growing the business to the next level when they can step back a bit. I can't help but be amazed that this model business has evolved so quickly and successfully under the leadership of two young men who weren't deterred by an initial obstacle. A simple conversation produced a wonderful and mutually beneficial outcome.

If I could do a backflip or even a chin-up in celebration I would have for these two enterprising young men. So I continued to watch with interest as the business grew. Four years after opening, the gymnasium is offering 24/7 access, and social media and word-of-mouth referrals see a steadily growing membership.

Dale has left and is pursuing other interests. Edward has introduced a new business partner, Gareth, and they operate a second gymnasium after purchasing Fit Republic in Golden Square, a suburb of nearby Bendigo. By marketing the two locations as 'sister gyms', there is the added attraction for members who commute for work between the two towns and are interested in accessing different trainers and programs. Edward is increasingly aware of the advantages of operating a business with access to a larger population base. 'Being in any business, not just the fitness industry, is tough and you definitely have to work harder with a small population base. I'm realising what a diverse community Castlemaine is; we're not just catering for 9 to 5 workers,' says Edward. He is also mindful of the threat of a competitor offering new facilities.

Consequently, Maine Fitness has been self-investing in improving the interior, replacing equipment, and offering more diverse activities. 'We now have a premier Martial Arts Academy and four other fitness classes on offer, everything from boxing to yoga.' 'During 2019 we sacrificed our Castlemaine profits to make sure we have a strong future,' Edward explains, 'and we're lucky we have a great landlord who understands and works with us.'

In March 2020 they were planning improvements to the exterior of the building to ensure they maintain a high profile. Their landlord, Glenn Guest, was equally excited. 'I'll be paying for the capital improvements, but it will be reflected in their lease payments,' he said. 'They have some good ideas.'

Sadly, those ideas were put on hold. It is no secret that the gym industry has been hard hit by the coronavirus. While the doors were forced to close and only briefly reopened in late-June, an online platform was quickly produced to keep members motivated and engaged in daily workouts. 'Although our memberships are on hold, we have leased out all our gym equipment for members to complete their workouts at home,' Edward said. He is still optimistic. 'I think people have become more health conscious through this pandemic.' Thankfully he and Gareth have a lot of energy and enthusiasm and, with strong support from the local community, will get back on track soon.

www.mainefitness.com.au

Determined

Determined, persistent, never gives up ...

This describes so many businesspeople I have interviewed. I am in awe of the obstacles they faced in getting started and how they overcome challenges that continue to come their way. Financial obstacles are particularly prevalent in the start-up and growth phases, and I love the creative ways they found to forge ahead regardless.

'Aim to be the top 10 per cent of any industry and you will do well.'

Pork farmer Tom Smith has learnt to anticipate what challenges and opportunities lie ahead in this industry and has carefully planned for family members with the benefit of succession planning.

'The staff here are wonderful. We had to keep them safe.'

During the COVID-19 panic buying that hit supermarkets, Brendan Blake had to find a way to feed the local population and also keep his staff and customers safe.

'I tested each sample by washing and testing for shrinkage before deciding on what was the right weight, stretch and durability for Skibo.'

With a preference for Australian made, Helenmary Macleod, founder of Skibo based in the Western District of Victoria, had to walk the streets of Melbourne to find a manufacturer willing to take on small runs.

'We support each other to exceed targets.'

With the past experience of being an Armenian refugee fleeing war-torn Ethiopia, Sebastian Parsegian was determined to also escape the city with his family by taking on a successful and award-winning business, Swan Hill Toyota.

'Take a chance – and work hard when you do!'

Likewise, Mandy Strong from Sunshine Iris Nursery in New South Wales was determined to prove to her husband that the nursery was more than a hobby, and she did!

In countless ways you must be determined to be successful in business.

Kia Ora Piggery

Tom Smith, Kia-Ora Piggery

'Aim to be the top 10 per cent of any industry and you will do well,' advises Tom Smith from Yarrawalla in North Central Victoria. Supported by wife Val and their children, the Smith family has transformed a traditional family farm into five companies that employ over 40 full-time staff to care for 2000 sows and their piglets. By milling and mixing all their stock feed, they have complete control from farrowing to finish.

As pigs were always a small part of his father's mixed farming activities, Tom was familiar with caring for them in what could be seen now as a primitive way. When he and Val married in 1971, a $40,000 loan was sought to build that component of the business but rejected by their bank at the time. Rural Finance also rejected the application suggesting it was too big a risk. Fortunately, the family were supportive.

With keen business intuition and a willingness to experiment, Tom's dad encouraged them to take full advantage of any assistance on offer. Purchasing the pigs was funded with the assistance of a stock agency veto over stock. Gippsland was experiencing drought, so the Smiths were also able to increase cash flow through hay sales and establish their new business with 100 sows.

'Oddly enough,' Tom reflects, 'several years later with the piggery functioning, we applied again for a loan to Rural Finance, and they knocked us back because we were in a good enough position to borrow from the commercial banks.'

The government at the time saw pigs as a potential industry and invested considerable money through the Department of Agriculture. 'This benefited us enormously,' says Tom. 'Department staff helped us to select breeding stock; they had an engineer on staff to design shedding, nutritionists to assist with the feed formulations, absolutely top veterinarians, pathologists and field officers. It was an incredible time of development. The industry has been very good to us.'

In 2016 there was an estimated $8 million of capital improvements on the books, indicating the Smith family don't operate by halves. 'There has never been a time when we have said we want to get bigger,' admits Tom, 'it has just evolved. All increases have been about improving.'

It also goes without saying that a lot of hard work and sacrifice helped their business to 'evolve'. Val has worked right from the beginning in the farrowing and training areas of the business and says she learned to ask 'lots of questions'. Their children were brought up to be independent. 'They got themselves ready for school, made their own lunches and beds from prep year onwards,' Val explains. She would leave the piggery in time to take them to the school bus. 'Life was a lot simpler for families back then. Kids entertained themselves.'

Instilling a strong work ethic has had positive outcomes for their now adult children. Their sons, Jarad and Caleb, are actively involved and each one is buying a portion of the business while daughter Jeannie and her husband lease some land and farm in their own right. Another daughter, Kellie, is a veterinarian and part owner of a practice in Eaglehawk.

Attracting good staff was a major challenge as their companies expanded. In 2010, Tom advertised in the *Manilla Times* attracting four quality staff. It made a significant difference. They now have 22 workers from the Philippines on their books. 'Working with pigs is a chosen career path in the Philippines,' explains Tom. 'Although not quite at a formal Australian veterinary standard, they are well educated in this industry and have a positive attitude to their work.'

As the business and family has simultaneously grown, succession planning has been at the back of Tom's mind. He knew there must be a better way than what he experienced with his father and four brothers. A partnership with one brother and his father existed until 1994 when it became time to move in different directions. Tom took on the piggery and the other brother took much of the land previously owned by their parents.

'For succession, my dad's idea was an insurance policy to cover the payout on his death with my brother and I paying the premium,' Tom explains. 'The property was valued and that value divided into five and the value increased equivalent to CPI each year. Upon reflection I think it would have been better settled when my brother and I first took control of the farming activities.

'All along Val and I have told our children there is no such thing as an inheritance,' says Tom. 'Kids in this day and age are in a better position to earn more.' Having said that, Tom admits that they have already given the kids their portion of the inheritance. 'It was easy to do. The returns (lease payments) on what the boys haven't paid for on our death goes to charity until purchased entirely. As a future owner of the company you have to be active in the company,' he adds. With the saying 'three generations from riches to rags' in mind, Tom's theory is that you will always have a second generation if the potential owners have to commit financially and be active in management.

Tom believes one of the best decisions he made in his career was the setting up of an advisory board, providing the family with an outside perspective. 'It was important for us to recognise the strengths in the boys and give them freedom to speak their mind, not just be a father-son relationship,' says Tom, who is also clear on his role as he starts to contemplate retirement.

No doubt the transition from a family farm partnership into a more complex company environment – that includes Kia-Ora Piggery, Kia-Ora Breeding, Walla Environmental Solutions (waste products), Sixth Gralloch Holdings (employment service company), and Goldfield Pork (wholesaling pork) – hasn't been without its bumps and challenges, both financially and emotionally. Fortunately, Tom's history of making good decisions has stood them in good stead.

In 2009/10, despite the pork industry shrinking 30% while Tom and Val were investing millions of dollars, they managed to retain the confidence of their bank manager. 'It is extra tough when pork prices are down, and grain prices are up,' says Tom. 'This has happened on several occasions, making it tough for all producers.'

A touch of competitiveness has encouraged Tom to take up benchmarking opportunities along the way. Thanks to their hard work, the Smith family is now a competitive player in the pork industry and ranked within the top three of their industry. In 2018 the business received a Victorian Regional Achievement and Community Award in recognition of the diversity and inclusion of their workforce, bringing positive publicity to the local community.

A firm believer in utilising whatever is available to you, Tom has put SPC Ardmona waste products to good use, feeding the contents to the stock and recycling the tin. This required over a million-dollar investment to set up the process; 18,000 pallets of tins over 18 months, recycling up to 50 tonne a day has made it worthwhile.

Always keen to innovate, a major project in 2018 was the installation of a biogas system to take advantage of the huge amounts of pig affluent generated onsite. Tom was excited. It has the capacity to reduce greenhouse emissions by 81% and generate more than 115% of the site's electricity needs, with the excess potentially being sold into the power grid as a greenhouse gas offset.

In 2020 I ask how it turned out. 'Yes, it is generating electricity, but it was a big learning process,' Tom admits. 'If you want to invent something, then you have to be prepared for the extra cost.'

Tom is sounding decidedly cheerful. 'Succession has happened!' he announces. As previously agreed, the two boys are taking over the management of the businesses and are buying in with the assistance of loans from their father. 'All businesses need to be paying attention to succession planning,' he reiterates. 'Continuity is important. We need to target leading figures in the business, it doesn't have to be family.'

He hesitates when I ask if he has officially retired. 'Well, I'm on the farm still, running 1200 ewes, and enjoying being able to travel when I can,' he clarifies. On a more sombre note, recent global challenges have impacted on the pork industry. It started with African swine fever and the Smiths ramped up their existing bio-security procedures even further. Then came a downturn in turnover due to closed restaurants and a lack of Chinese tourists during coronavirus restrictions.

'Physically there has been little impact, other than social distancing and scheduling starting times, smokos and lunches so the amenities can cope in this regard. Financially, areas are being hit badly. One week we had to freeze pork due to having nowhere to sell it.'

Tom is equally concerned for the region with wool and barley profits also being affected. No doubt he will be involved in finding ways to help mitigate the impact.

TOM'S TOP BUSINESS TIPS:

- Aim for the top 10% of any industry.
- Have a vision.
- Utilise any resources available to you including professional advice.
- Communicate openly and often.
- Your staff are your biggest asset. Care for them and they will care for you.
- Organise your succession, whether with your family or even top managerial staff early in your business path. The sooner the better with family. They then know what to expect.

Maxi IGA

Brendan Blake, Maxi IGA

In 2020 we have witnessed scenes of empty supermarket shelves never seen before in our lifetime. An obsession with toilet paper, rice and pasta became an acute issue as people worldwide were urged by governments to 'stay at home' during coronavirus restrictions. A spotlight has been shone on local manufacturers and suppliers in every rural and regional community, creating a new level of loyalty and appreciation.

Brendan Blake grew up in supermarkets. By Year 11 he was managing one of his father's stores every weekend in the Melbourne suburb of Kew. Twenty years ago, Brendan purchased Castlemaine Maxi IGA in regional Victoria and officially became a storeowner. Despite his extensive experience Brendan says he has never seen such massive change as has been experienced during the COVID-19 restrictions. The good news is that local independent supermarkets have become even more highly valued in their communities and Brendan has become an accidental 'foodie' in the public eye.

'It's been change like I've never seen before,' he admitted when I spoke with him in early June 2020. 'Suppliers have been unable to supply. Customers have bought out the store. We've had to learn some quick tricks.' Brendan does not take his duties lightly. Maxi IGA is the major food supplier in the City of Castlemaine with a population of around 8000 and a further 10,000 in nearby smaller towns. He employs around 230 local people.

Customers had the choice of shopping in the closest regional city of Bendigo where the big chain supermarkets operate in abundance, before travel restrictions directed all locals to the Maxi IGA and one other smaller independent IGA store in Castlemaine.

'I'm responsible for supplying food to the local population,' says Brendan. 'I have to go and find food' ... *and toilet paper* I silently add. Almost as if he heard me, Brendan launches into the story of how he sourced a semi load of toilet paper from a friend who just happens to be a toilet paper manufacturer.

He has also reached out to many small businesses. 'As soon as COVID happened I told the local providers that I would support them. For instance, Edmund at The Mill had to shut his cafe down overnight. We sell his Coffee Basics coffee beans and help his cash flow.'

Enthusiastically Brendan steers me around the store pointing out new shelf displays of local products. Everything from locally made soaps to honey, puddings, and smallgoods. 'We've always stocked local produce; the range is driven by what people want, but I put the call out so others could join while there is no foot traffic past their stores. He comments on the rejection of overseas products. 'Consumers are looking for Australian made.'

One major issue, still relevant two months on, has been the difficulty in sourcing staples such as rice and flour. Thinking laterally, Brendan approached restaurant–wholesalers to purchase their bulk products, for which they had a depleted market. Product was then repackaged into one-kilogram packs.

Unlike other supermarkets that purchase packaged meat from the big distributors in Melbourne, Castlemaine Maxi IGA buys whole carcasses and runs its own in-house butcher department. This turned out to be a massive advantage during the restrictions. 'We never ran out of mincemeat,' Brendan tells me proudly. 'We had bucket loads while all the big supermarket chains sold out.'

Perhaps the most surprising element for Brendan has been the massive surge in social media support for the store and himself personally. 'We started to inform people on Facebook. We have rice, we have pasta.' These simple announcements soon escalated to higher levels. 'I enjoy cooking. I cook for the family every night, so I started sharing recipes and doing product reviews in the store. It's like a blog.'

While the store had maintained a Facebook page for five years its static following quickly tripled. Clearly a numbers man, Brendan informs me that the Castlemaine store now has 1666 followers. Without support or training he admits to doing all this on his iPhone as he walks around the store. Judging by the comments, his followers love it.

'I've become a social media junkie!' he exclaims. And there's another exceptionally good reason. 'Previously our marketing catalogue took up to 10 days to publish and distribute. Facebook and email are instant. It is a tenth of our previous advertising cost and has a far wider reach,' says Brendan.

While saving money in some areas he has also invested in others. 'The staff here are wonderful. We had to keep them safe. I made a phone call at nine one morning to a plastic manufacturer and by 2 pm we had plastic sneeze guards installed on every workstation. The big chain stores followed our lead.'

Automatic hand-sanitiser dispensers and social-distancing markers on the floors are here to stay. New lighting and signage are brightening up the store. Brendan points out each and every little improvement explaining the detail to me. Local trades are being employed and supported.

I am exhausted by the time we complete a tour of my local supermarket after looking at it in an entirely different light. Hands on and methodical, Brendan is constantly straightening products and chatting with staff along the way. Showing incredible willpower, I have resisted tasting samples at the new yogurt bar. A selection of Georgina's cakes was ready and waiting for Brendan's daily visit to the in-house bakery. Apparently, he had to photograph the previous day's vanilla slice being cut on the tray as well as taste it. Judging by the friendly jibes, a fair portion did not make it to the shelves.

Oblivious to my lack of culinary skills Brendan provides me with tips of exquisite products that I must try. Of far more use, he provides me with a valuable insight into what has gone on behind the scenes in a business selling essential products during this extraordinary time. The value of local manufacturers and producers has been clearly highlighted.

Like everyone else, Brendan Blake did not anticipate 2020 being such a massive challenge but admits that much good has come out of it. 'It has been a rebirthing of the whole business. It has been a good experience.' Will this appreciation for local suppliers and retailers last, I wonder?

Brendan is adamant, 'People will not forget.'

www.facebook.com/MaxiIGACastlemaine

Skibo Australia

Helenmary Macleod, Skibo Australia

Helenmary Macleod grew up on a farm and married a farmer but she always loved the idea of selling things to make people happy. Being regularly away from the farm, especially during cropping in summer, wasn't an option but then came the idea for Skibo Australia. Not only has this addressed a gap in the market, the skivvies are made in Australia from 100% cotton jersey and attract seasonal winter sales – fitting in perfectly with life on the farm.

For younger readers, except perhaps golfers and snow skiers, skivvies may be an alien concept but being a country gal, it is music to my ears. The skivvies I recall from my 1970s youth have long gone from the shops. Skibo also excites me because its products are manufactured in Melbourne, a rarity that deserved further exploration.

In 2019 I caught up with Helenmary who lives with husband Duncan on their cropping property near Willaura in western Victoria. Helenmary started by paying tribute to women who prompted her to start Skibo Australia in 1998.

'A number of pioneering women from the Western District with their own unique fashion brands were a great influence and inspired me to get started. We had no business forums back in those days, but they were very generous with their advice. They told me to look for what was missing rather than what is already available on the market.'

Helenmary didn't have to look far. 'I found it ridiculous that you couldn't buy decent skivvies and wondered why we can't make them in Australia.' She decided that this could be her entry into the retail world, albeit in a small way. 'Duncan was very supportive. We put a budget aside that we were prepared to lose if necessary. We just decided to have a crack at this and see what happens.'

Not having a fashion or manufacturing background didn't deter Helenmary. She knew what she wanted, and she had lots of encouragement from the local women. After a Google search the couple travelled to Melbourne to source the material and meet with pattern makers, fabric printers and manufacturers. Some of their tasks were easier than others. 'I was determined not to go offshore for the manufacturing, but it was difficult to find someone prepared to do short runs. We were very green and, in the beginning, didn't ask all the right questions.'

It was a chance discussion with her hairdresser that put Helenmary in touch with a company that does short manufacturing runs for a women's fashion franchise. They also assisted her to find the right cotton jersey by sending samples for her to experiment with at home. 'That took a lot of research as well,' Helenmary admits. 'I tested each sample by washing and testing for shrinkage before deciding on what was the right weight, stretch and durability for Skibo.' In hindsight, Helenmary says the key is to find businesses interested in what you are doing, prepared to work with you, and willing to start off small scale to see how it goes. 'It also helps if they have an understanding that you live in the country and can't pop in to double-check,' she adds.

With a suitable fabric selected, Helenmary designed the patterns and chose the colours. 'When everything was ready to go for our first run the manufacturer asked if I wanted to print 20 rolls or more when we only wanted one or two as a trial. Thankfully he agreed to put it through as a sample run and to take it from there.'

The business name came from Helenmary's research into her maiden family history. The Sutherlands have a connection with Skibo Castle in Scotland. It also had a nice synergy with her products being skivvies.

In its first decade, Skibo built a loyal customer base through mail order catalogues and seven field days across Tasmania, Victoria, South Australia and New South Wales, often with children in tow. 'I love seeing customers coming back each year and field days can be very profitable if you choose the right ones,' Helenmary says. Duncan's engineering skills ensured that she had a good set-up for those field days. 'Everything fits into the back of a Falcon station wagon – the poles, lattice for the shelving, and the skivvies in bags. We've now started using the back of the ute with a canopy.'

But then customers started telling her she should go online. Knowing very little about the internet, Helenmary went back into research mode and sought professional support. The first website proved to be cumbersome so Helenmary sought more advice. The move to Wordpress means she can do a lot of the updating and customers can see the amount of stock in hand. At the start of each season Helenmary meets with her website designer to review the site and rings her if she has problems. It's proving to be a good arrangement.

'Some customers were dubious in the beginning and preferred to give me their credit card details over the phone but now people are much more comfortable with shopping online.'

Heading into winter, Helenmary is busy adjusting colours and styles so there is always fresh stock for customers. Five years ago she introduced a children's line of skivvies. 'We started with small numbers using the scraps from the adult skivvies but the last year they're really taken off and we're now doing bigger runs.'

While word-of-mouth referrals work well for her business, Helenmary has slowly ventured into Facebook and Instagram. She is able to proudly display the Made in Australia logo and can claim that her quality skivvies stand the test of time, something that goes well with rural customers. Skibo is fortunate to be able to manufacture short runs in the hundreds, one of the advantages of onshore manufacturing. They're housed on the farm in an old building that has served multiple purposes over the generations and is now referred to as Skivvies House! Internet orders are parcelled up and driven 40 kilometres into Willaura to catch the 2 pm post.

Duncan and Helenmary were recently excited to become grandparents – and Skibo continues to work in well with family and farm life. Although Helenmary once shut down sales to take a year off, she returned with renewed enthusiasm and has no plans to sell the business. She sounded a little unsettled when I suggested this to her. 'Skibo is profitable and it's good to have extra income,' Helenmary says. 'I keep going because it is mine and getting off the farm and meeting people is good for me.'

Well, maybe not so much in 2020, a year that could not have been predicted. No field days to attend this year but at least she can still sell online and there is always something to do on the farm. The new Skibo Australia range was launched after they finished their scheduled sheep work. 'I'm excited about this year's range and believe it will appeal to women of all ages.' Helenmary admitted that the web page had some major issues at the end of last year and had to be rebuilt – audible groan. Just what she needed over the summer break!

This year is a special milestone for Skibo Australia. 'We celebrate our 21st birthday in 2020,' Helenmary said 'We have a few plans in mind.' Watch this space, in other words!

www.skibo.net.au

Swan Hill Toyota

Sebastian Parsegian, Swan Hill Toyota

Sebastian Parsegian has had two lucky escapes in his lifetime. The first was 40 years ago as an 11-year-old Armenian refugee fleeing war-torn Ethiopia. The second was when he and wife Rebecca left their jobs in Melbourne and moved to Swan Hill in country Victoria to become award-winning business owners.

If leaving his job selling used cars in Melbourne was a concern at the time, it certainly isn't now. With multiple trophies lining his office, including the prestigious 2016 Toyota Australian Dealer of the Year, Seb looks very comfortable as both a business owner and resident of a country town. 'We're out of the rat race,' explains Seb. 'In Melbourne you don't even know who your neighbour is. We have a sense of belonging here and I have an extra 70 hours a month up my sleeve. No travel and friendlier work hours.'

Having wisely invested their hard-earned wages into property, Seb and Rebecca were in the fortunate position of being able to buy into an existing business in Swan Hill in 2007. With their son aged 10, it was a great time to move to the country. 'We turned up at the football one Sunday at Lake Boga, where we bought a house, and were welcomed with open arms. Through children and sport you automatically get to connect with people.'

Business wise, Swan Hill Toyota had already enjoyed some success and they were able to invest just as it relocated to new purpose-built premises on the Murray Valley Highway leading into Swan Hill. That success has now doubled. Since taking over, the business has increased its staff numbers from 14 to 34. The sales figures reflect why. When Seb and Rebecca took over 27 vehicles were sold a month; which quickly went to 50, and is now 70.

A new location would have contributed to this success but more so the culture. What makes this rural-based business so competitive at a national level? Quietly spoken Seb believes that sharing his 25 years' experience of selling cars with staff helped to increase sales straightway. Rebecca also brought with her the experience of working in the car industry, and has since become the principal dealer of Swan Hill KIA located conveniently across the road.

They continue to invest in staff through the Toyota franchise's extensive training program. 'We support each other to exceed targets,' says Seb. Everyone gets a KPI bonus regardless of the department they work in, encouraging teamwork and innovation. 'Customers are our guests. The relationship is definitely more important than the sale. It's all about the experience.'

Fast forward to 2020. Seb is away from his desk when I call in early March but Gavin his friendly Sales Manager is only too happy to chat.

'Seb is encouraging staff to step up more,' he confides. 'He is working on the business more than in it these days.' Talking with Gavin before COVID restrictions it is clear the team is already proactive in monitoring their customers and the external environment. 'Our target markets changed a bit because of the economy and drought,' he explains. 'While that has affected our farmer customers, we have been able to build up the private market more. We need to be adaptive by changing our strategy.'

By moving their used cars to a new site on the opposite side of the highway they've increased sales and also impacted positively on Kia's sales and their other business managed by Rebecca.

When coronavirus restrictions were imposed later that month, Gavin says they had to adapt just like everyone else. 'We're doing a bit more online and we've brought in social-distancing protocols. Supply of stock will be a concern in future, but we're all in the same boat.

'It really is a great place to work and the business has such a great reputation. Seb and the business are still heavily involved in the community,' says Gavin.

When I first met Seb and Rebecca, they were extremely proud of being announced as the 2016 Toyota Australian Dealer of the Year over all the metropolitan-based franchises. On four occasions they had won Rural Dealer of the Year; now they had received acknowledgement at the highest level. 'We were so pleased for our staff and customers,' recalls Seb, reliving the announcement made at the 2016 gala dinner in Melbourne.

In 2020 it was a very different experience but exciting, nonetheless. In an online announcement in April, Toyota announced that Swan Hill Toyota had won their ninth President's Award in 10 years. 'It was a massive achievement for Swan Hill – we punch well above our weight,' adds Rebecca. 'A number of businesses are operating at a national level.'

Yes, Seb and Rebecca wholeheartedly agree; moving to Swan Hill was a great decision.

www.swanhilltoyota.com.au

Sunshine Iris Nursery

Mandy Strong, Sunshine Iris Nursery

Usually the children are encouraged to take on the family business, but in the case of Sunshine Iris Nursery near Lockhart in New South Wales, it was the opposite. What started as a logical step into the business world for agronomist-trained Elissa Strong became problematic when she went back to study in 2017, leaving her mother Mandy to pick, pack and post.

Much to my son's delight I was invited to lunch at the home of daredevil X-Games and freestyle motorcycle rider Jackson Strong in 2018. However, I was not there to meet the international superstar, I was there to catch up with Mandy Strong, Jackson's quietly spoken mother and co-owner of Sunshine Iris Nursery.

Driving on to the Strong's 8000-hectare cereal cropping farm near Lockhart in the Riverina district of New South Wales, I immediately spotted two distinct differences to every other farming property I've visited. First and foremost, there is Jackson's elaborate training track, and alongside a fenced paddock of flowering irises of all colours and descriptions. Quite by accident I timed my visit in October, right in the middle of flowering season!

While she has always been a part of the family farming enterprise – and the 'number two header driver' until their eldest son Toby was old enough to take over – Mandy's main profession was teaching. It was in 2013, around the time of her retirement, that her daughter Elissa spotted a nearby iris business for sale. With Elissa's agronomist training and Mandy's love of gardening it seemed like a good opportunity. 'Let's do this,' Elissa told her mother. So, they did. 'My husband thought it a ridiculous idea,' Mandy admits, 'but we've proven the business is profitable.'

At this point I was embarrassed to admit my lack of gardening knowledge so Mandy sets me straight. It turns out there are over 600 varieties of drought-resistant, disease-free irises and they multiply each year. Perfect for Australian gardens, which is why Sunshine Irises has sales to every state and territory. Walking through the allotment I saw firsthand the range of colours and sizes, making it a collector's paradise and attracting many repeat customers.

Mandy pulled out her smart phone and opened up the Shopify app they use in their online business. Even though they advertise that orders cannot be processed during the flowering season from September to November, there were already 108 orders logged and awaiting delivery. Each order is clearly identified by a photo of the iris being purchased and each iris in the allotment is carefully labelled making the selections easy.

'Basically, we pick, pack and post,' Mandy explains. 'Shopify is perfect for this type of business and prints all the reports we need.' Prepaid bags are purchased and posted through their local post office in Lockhart. Extra care needs to be taken with orders to Western Australia and Tasmania due to quarantine laws. 'We treat them with a special spray and have extra paperwork. It's not hard once you're in the system and, being an agronomist, Elissa set it up.'

Two years into the business and the daughter–mother duo purchased another iris collection, this time from Yarrawonga, adding significantly to their stock. They also introduced 80 varieties of daylilies. The business is significantly growing.

While the iris and lily bulbs are the main product, the blooms are also sold during flowering season at a market in Wagga Wagga.

In 2017, when Elissa returned to study and found it impossible to actively contribute, Mandy took on the business – but not without support. She invited her twin sister Margie, who lives in Canberra, to become the new partner. 'I do all the physical stuff and Margie does the books, blogs for our website, and runs social media and works behind-the-scenes,' says Mandy. They also have an employee, conveniently Mandy's next-door neighbour, who comes and helps pack every Monday. University students assist with weeding on a seasonal basis.

And sometimes matters just go your way when you are surrounded by equally motivated businesspeople, albeit for very different purposes. Mandy reports that water for the irises is plentiful. Jackson's new training track required extra dirt, which was excavated from the dam creating a far greater storage capacity. An aerial video of the iris allotment for the Facebook page also came courtesy of her son's drone.

Apart from the occasional open day during the flowering season it is a solitary business but, well used to rural life, Mandy appears to relish it. Lucky, given the impact of coronavirus in 2020!

The internet has created sales well beyond her patch of rural bliss and she remains active in her local community of Lockhart. During February, the business donated a dollar for every iris sold to support BlazeAid volunteers assisting farmers with the bushfire recovery.

Showing a hint of why her son Jackson has become known as an innovator in the sporting world, Mandy believes that anyone can do well in business if they think outside the square and develop something that suits their interests and skill set. 'I've always been a gardener and love growing things,' she says. Best of all the business also provides an income independent of the farm, which apparently surprised a few people along the way.

MANDY'S TOP BUSINESS TIPS:

- Take the time to talk to your customers, even those not tech savvy.
- Take a chance – and work hard when you do!
- Enjoy what you are doing, and it doesn't become a chore.

  www.sunshineiris.com.au

Problem Solving

Entrepreneurs see a problem and love the challenge of solving it, as these stories demonstrate. History has shown time and time again, that meeting people's needs is the pathway to success, not a focus on the wealth creation that will naturally follow.

'For the first 15 years of my business I spent more time convincing people that raw food is an option; now it is about which brand is best.'

As a young veterinarian fresh out of university, Dr Bruce Syme developed a new raw food-based diet in response to the epidemic proportions of skin diseases and allergies presenting in cats and dogs at his surgery. Vets all Natural has grown from humble beginnings to forge new frontiers in the pet food industry.

'We've created something that can solve a global issue.'

Such was the case of Trent Small when he experienced the destruction of Cyclone Yasi in 2011. Extended power outages got this Queensland businessman thinking about what could best help communities in times of crisis. Solar Relief was the result.

'I love experimenting and seeing things grow.'

When presented with problems faced by his local council including disposing of green waste, an outbreak of mastitis in local dairy cattle, and paddocks suffering high salinity, Travis Howard came up with a great solution that evolved into a business, Redgum Organics.

'We're seeing the start of a big disruption. It's not about government creating change, it is up to us.'

Physical Education teacher Jarrod Robinson utilised technology to better engage his rural students for their Victorian curriculum exam. He became known as The PE Geek and created a global business opportunity in ConnectedPE. I love that Jarrod's problem-solving skills took him from the tiny township of Boort in Central Victoria to Dubai and, ultimately, the world.

'We want children to understand that they're not stupid, they just learn differently, and give them the tools to cope in their normal school environment.'

Wholebrain founder Denise Smith knows firsthand what it's like to be a right-brain learner in a left-brain-orientated education system. She has spent over a decade developing a specific font, phonics program and word lists to help young people with dyslexia to cope in the classroom.

Vets All Natural

Dr Bruce Syme, Vets All Natural, and Healthy Pets Veterinary Clinic

Twenty-five years ago, Dr Bruce Syme, a young veterinarian fresh out of university, developed a raw food-based diet in response to the epidemic proportions of skin diseases and allergies presenting in cats and dogs. Determined to take a holistic approach he relocated his pet food business and set up his own practice in Central Victoria. Today Vets All Natural products can be found on pet supply shelves in many countries.

Catching up with Bruce for a coffee at his home town of Guildford in 2018, we reminisced about how much has changed since 1999 when I drove into the bush to interview him the first time. Having just moved from Melbourne to start his own practice in a more receptive community, he had rented rooms behind a dog kennel business at Muckleford, a rural community between Castlemaine and Maldon. It was quite a challenging mud map I had to draw for the photographer to find him later that week.

I remember writing that Bruce was 'a new breed of vet with a passion'. His focus was on keeping pets healthy instead of treating the disease. That hasn't changed but much else has. For a start we are both older and wiser, the single vet practice has grown significantly, and there are now many more competitor brands on the shelves of retail outlets emulating the Vets All Natural products.

'I started on a wing and a prayer, just flying by the seat of my pants,' Bruce admits reflecting on both his practice and pet food manufacturing business. 'Things just grew and grew.' Two years after his move to Central Victoria, he was able to buy out an existing practice in nearby Castlemaine and farewell his remote location. As his pet-food business gained traction he also built a shed and rented a second one. 'It was quite rapid growth. I took on another vet and the head nurse as partners and we employed another full-time vet and support staff. I had to focus on the practice and relied on employees to look after the food manufacturing.'

When it came to finances, in the early days Bruce admits he was a novice. 'I wasn't financially motivated. If there was money in the bank, I thought things were going well.' His sounding board was a best friend who had studied commerce. As a young vet with a student debt, the banks weren't interested when he approached them to set up his own business. His father provided a loan – which Bruce is quick to confirm has been repaid including interest.

Bruce outlines three trigger points that forced him to study his business finances more closely. Starting a family at the same time he bought the Castlemaine practice in 2000 was the first; both brought more financial responsibilities. Second was the realisation that his pet-food manufacturing business was creating 80% of his income from a 20% output. 'I started paying more interest then,' he says. And, lastly, taking out a $1 million loan to build a new home for the growing practice with a fully equipped veterinary hospital in 2014.

Bruce admits that the veterinary industry is not as profitable as many would like to think. 'It's a rewarding but tough industry. In comparison to a doctor's surgery, the overheads are massive. As a clinic we provide everything, including two surgical theatres and all modern equipment including in-house blood testing, ultrasound, endoscopy and radiology.'

'I knew I couldn't muck around anymore,' says Bruce, who took on a business mentor and coach and signed up for a business management course. While it was important to understand his businesses he also found it frustrating that 'best practice' – as prescribed by the expert trainers – was focused on getting maximum profit. 'Ethics are not very profitable,' he admits. 'There is this horrible thing called integrity and emotional health.' While many vets are now refusing to visit properties for large animals because it is not profitable, Bruce believes it is part of their community service, and he gets to enjoy the beautiful countryside in the process.

On the bright side, as a result of all the training, he now knows exactly how much it costs to run the practice on an hourly basis and how much he has to earn to cover his debts. And, while it was important for him to remain hands-on in the rebranded Healthy Pets Veterinary Clinic, it was equally important for him to nurture the more lucrative Vets All Natural business and reassess his role in it. 'It's all about effort and return. I started analysing the retail pet market around the time of the big corporate mergers and realised it was important to get involved with the franchises. We started by getting our products into 15 stores through one franchise and now it is 120 stores.'

When it came to marketing Bruce sponsored many cat and dog shows and, in the early days, spent time on the lecture circuit, talking to fellow vets, animal breeders and owners. 'We targeted the key influencers and developed some core believers,' he explains, and it worked beautifully. He recalls that once a dog owner drove to his Castlemaine practice from Melbourne after a passer-by noticed her dog scratching. The passer-by suggested the dog owner google Vets All Natural and go see Dr Bruce Syme!

The irony of being successful is that your competitors quickly follow. 'For the first 15 years of my business I spent more time convincing people that raw food is an option; now it is about which brand is best,' says Bruce. All along he has paid attention to what customers need. Handling raw meat on its own was problematic so a line of dry grain mix products was introduced. New styles of packaging, including a peel and serve option, also helped keep Vets All Natural ahead of its competitors.

The dilemma of any business owner and parent is getting the right work–life balance and, on reflection, Bruce suspects he could have done better. Developing new product lines also required big investment. As a result, Vets All Natural has changed significantly. It is now a company with shareholders and operates from a head office in St Kilda Road, Melbourne, under the guidance of a general manager. Manufacturing is outsourced to three other businesses leaving the company to manage warehousing and distribution. 'Brand and intellectual property are our biggest assets,' Bruce says. 'We distribute nationwide and overseas to Japan and Singapore. Currently we are going into China with a massive deal; clean and green products are very big there.'

Surrounding himself with smart people has paid dividends for Bruce, who took on the position of Executive Director. 'I handed over a business with a $1 million annual turnover and they've increased it four times over.'

'One of the hardest things was letting go and trusting other people,' he admits; however, there have been many advantages. 'I was able to pull back from the marketing and focus on the science.' He also drives fewer kilometres and can spend three days a week in his veterinary practice, where his presence is important.

Shortly after working on a joint venture to develop a new product, Bruce was approached about selling the Vets All Natural pet food business to The Staughton Group, a family-owned fresh meat processor and manufacturer. 'The company is much bigger than us and when they put an offer on the table that ticked all the boxes it was an easy decision to make,' says Bruce. 'An exit strategy has always been in the back of my mind; I've been running the business for 26 years.'

In early 2020, I am interested to hear that it is a rolling buyout with 12 months still to complete. I ask Bruce more about the reasoning behind this strategy assuming that all the benefits are for the buyer. 'Yes, it was their preference,' he admits, 'but it works for us as well. We get to maintain a profit share arrangement over that timeframe and, because they have a much bigger market reach than us into the United States, we've also got a share of increased business and profit. Everyone can benefit in this type of arrangement.'

Bruce is called back to consult now and then but basically has stepped back from the pet food manufacturing business. 'Smiling and saying that was fun,' he adds.

Still a majority owner of the Healthy Pets Veterinary Clinic, he works two to three days a week. Coronavirus has not prevented pets from needing care. Safe practices have been put in place to protect clients and staff. And, finally, Bruce has hit his perfect work–life balance.

BRUCE'S TOP BUSINESS TIPS:

- Choose something that you enjoy.
- Do your homework and understand that the environment rapidly changes.
- Don't become blind to something you are passionate about. If you have a great idea, challenge it and get other people to challenge it as well.
- Get advice from people who know what they are doing.
- Take care of your physical and mental health.

  www.healthypetsvc.com.au

  www.vetsallnatural.com.au

Solar Relief

Trent Small, Solar Relief (photo supplied)

Cyclone Yasi's destructive path in 2011 provided an opportunity for Trent Small, an enterprising Townsville businessman, to put his creative thinking and practical skills into action. Hailed as an important tool for disaster relief, Solar Relief received the UNESCO Energy Globe Award in 2017 for its role in powering remote schools in Fiji following Cyclone Winston.

In February 2011, when tropical Cyclone Yasi wreaked its devastation across the South Pacific and made landfall in Townsville, Queensland, Trent Small and his family were one of thousands affected by power outages for days.

'We were all rushing out to get ice and generators to try and save our food,' recalls Trent. 'At the same time, I kept looking at my neighbour's roof full of solar panels. It seemed crazy that no one could access the power they were generating.'

With this challenge in mind, Trent set about solving a problem that has changed his life. Having been through what he calls the 'school of hard knocks' Trent was well prepared for such a challenge. 'When I left school, I started a traineeship with a steel company but I always wanted to start my own business, so I also studied some law and economics subjects at university.' By age 21 he was self-employed and hasn't looked back.

When Cyclone Yasi hit, Trent was proprietor of an established business, Absolute Building Supplies. This helped immensely in his new quest to create a portable solar power solution. Because of the Federal Government's existing solar scheme, he had a good understanding of solar technology. 'I'd already looked into it and educated myself,' explains Trent, who went on to sell a half dozen of the grid systems before deciding that it didn't meet his vision for a sustainable future. 'There were too many people with a smash-and-grab mentality and over-inflated prices,' he shrugs. 'I chose to walk away.'

Trent was now focused on a portable solar product that could be quickly deployed anywhere in the world at times of natural disaster and crisis. Almost every week since Yasi, Trent sees instances where his portable solar power pack could make a difference. At the time of our interview world news was reporting on a power outage at a Uganda Hospital. 'There were three deaths in three hours,' recalls Trent. 'This could be totally preventable.'

A crucial aspect of being portable was the storage of power. He believed the answer was to develop a diverse product that could be charged in a number of different ways using solar and alternators off a car or generator, as well as be used as a UPS unit and off mains power. Even wind power was thrown into the mix.

In true Australian style he started experimenting with a battery box in an esky, before progressing to custom manufacturing moulds with input provided by the Australian Defence Force and Emergency Services. The non-reflective solar panels weigh four kilograms and fold down to 580 x 580 millimetres. The total weight of a patented PPS unit starts at 40 kilograms.

Up until this point Trent has invested his own time and money into the product development while his original business, Absolute Building Supplies, is developing a complementary product; fully recycled, Lego-style building materials to provide quick and ready shelter following a disaster.

Once Solar Relief hit the point of commercialisation and met all the stringent safety regulation standards, it became a separate company and took pre-orders. Trent is also seeking investors and talking with potential partners such as the United Nations and Rotary International, organisations that can help take the product where it is most needed around the world.

Not only is he passionate about disaster relief, he has a vision for a clean sustainable future for developing countries. 'I've got a product which I now believe is part of the solution to solve world energy poverty,' he explains. 'There's over 2.6 billion people who don't have access to reliable electricity and another 1.3 billion who have no access to electricity. We can take solar relief anywhere in the world and put down on the ground in a helicopter in any disaster area.'

Powering communication, lighting and medical devices in a disaster area can clearly save lives. Not only that, poverty can be alleviated. Trent explains how he and some colleagues recently delivered three PPS units to schools and villages in remote Fiji devastated by Cyclone Winston. 'Without power the school couldn't even print out exams for the kids to do,' Trent says. 'Our Facebook site lights up every day with hits from all around the world, people are crying out for this product.' In 2017 he flew to Iran to accept a UNESCO Energy Globe Award for Solar Relief's role in powering remote schools in Fiji following Cyclone Winston. 'This was incredible global recognition, with 176 countries in attendance.'

In 2020, at a time when so many Australian communities are experiencing extended power cuts due to fire, floods or cyclones, it seems timely to catch up with Trent.

Solar Relief continues to operate successfully alongside his core business, Absolute Building Supplies. Eighteen months ago, he brought on board a new business partner, Matthew, to help manage his multiple businesses. But Solar Relief remains Trent's passion. Over the past two years Trent has worked on developing and manufacturing their battery system. In November 2019 he excitedly announced the new PPS with 13 kWh battery storage, more than what is provided by a standard Tesla Powerwall.

'We've come a long way from our first systems which only had 0.8 kWh of battery storage,' Trent reflects. 'We also now have a wind turbine-charging option so the unit can be charged with both solar and wind. The world will benefit from our tenacity!

'It's about to get exciting in 2020,' he tells me. 'We've been doing a lot of trial work and some pretty exciting stuff with the Australian Defence Department – which is now about to take off. We've created something that can really solve a global issue.'

www.solar-relief.com

Redgum Organics

Travis Howard, Redgum Organics

A common attribute of an entrepreneur is their desire to find a solution to a problem. Another is that they often don't fit the school system.

It was no surprise that Travis Howard of Cohuna used to be easily distracted at school. 'All I could think about was farming,' he admits. When the family dairy farm was sold in 2006 Travis contracted his skills out and kept his eyes open for opportunities.

When the Ganawarra Shire was trying to decide how to dispose of its green waste collection in 2009, Cr Goulding approached Travis with an idea. As a result of that initial conversation, Travis established Redgum Organics, a business beneficial for the shire, the environment, and farmers.

Travis started buying green waste from the Gannawarra Shire. His idea was to relocate it to dairy farms requiring bedding for their cows prone to mastitis and other conditions exacerbated by lying on the wet ground. A big tick for the shire; an even bigger tick for the dairy industry. Travis then collects the waste – now further enriched – and composts it in windrows over a six-month period before sifting it into a product suitable for vegetable gardens, lawns, and pasture enhancement. Another big tick for his customers.

A field day sparked the original idea and YouTube and the internet provided the rest of the knowledge that Travis needed to get his business started. 'I love experimenting and seeing things grow,' says Travis. He needed help to get started and pays credit to his father for being a great business mentor. The farming community also got behind him. John Keely and other local farmers have allowed him to make use of their land to process the compost. Travis continues to move his enterprise around the Cohuna district, utilising land too salty for the farmers to use. In return for the use of the land he spreads compost and improves the soil so that farmers will once again be able to use their paddocks.

It is proving to be a profitable business. Travis started processing 80 tonnes of waste annually on the ground; four years later it was 2500 tonnes. Seven years on and he is processing 4000 tonnes and employing a local person three days a week. As both Travis and his employee have young families, it suits them to work part time allowing them the flexibility to share childcare responsibilities with their partners. 'Having someone working with me has taken the pressure off,' says Travis, but admits that taking the step from working solo to being an employer was a big one. 'I never realised there was so much paperwork with super and tax.' His accountant was duly enlisted to help set up that side of the business.

And Travis has not finished yet. His domestic market has grown significantly since we first spoke in 2016. Travis is pleased to update me in 2020 that he has now purchased a farm outside Cohuna from which Redgum Organics continues to operate. He's also running cattle in a semi-feed-lot situation, creating compost with the assistance of old hay purchased from local farmers. Having decided there is too much plastic in the green waste supplied through council transfer stations, Travis has provided local residents and commercial gardeners with a free drop-off station at his property. 'It's free but they have to separate it. Leaves, clippings, branches all have to be put into separate piles. I've also got a spot for soil.' He says up to 20 or 30 people drop off material each day, all generated by a Facebook post on his personal page and word of mouth. 'We're going to put some signage up but just haven't got around to it yet.'

In other exciting news Travis has also established a new depot at Barham. While contract working on a farm he forged a relationship with two sawmills in the district. Since December 2018 Travis has been pumping manure from a big dairy farm in Barham on to sawdust and scrap chips. 'I reckon there is about 3000 tonnes sitting there cooking and getting ready to go. I'm hoping to start spreading on paddocks in the autumn break.'

With the drought slowing the paddock work, Travis is currently working solo in the business but will happily scale up again when conditions allow. And, of course, machinery is always important. 'I've bought a little tipper for deliveries to our domestic customers.'.

Redgum Organics is one of the fortunate businesses in 2020. 'When the restrictions to stay at home started in March I sold out of my soil because a lot of people started to grow their own vegetables and get out in the garden.' Reflecting on this experience, Travis has now decided to start growing vegetables on the business site to showcase the value of his soil and compost. Always a new idea to implement.

www.facebook.com/Redgum-Organics

ConnectedPE

Jarrod Robinson, ConnectedPE

A love of sharing knowledge and an ability to problem solve led to a unique business opportunity for Jarrod Robinson who is inspiring physical education teachers worldwide to get better results for their students through use of technology. Known as The PE Geek, Jarrod took on a six-month world tour in 2016 and launched a global conference in Dubai.

Jarrod's exciting diversion into business kicked off in 2012 while he was teaching Year 12 students in physical education at Boort, a P–12 school that services a small agricultural region in Victoria. Growing up in a similar rural community in the Goulburn Valley, Jarrod's parents had encouraged him to be resourceful from a young age.

Long before 'tech was cool' and, despite no formal ICT training, he recognised the value of technology and sitting on his couch at home of an evening designed a mobile app complete with podcasts, videos, articles and social elements to better engage his students for their Victorian curriculum exam. In the first year this free app was downloaded over 15,000 times by VCE students' statewide. Jarrod had hit on a winner.

'This success inspired me to build on the app suite, venturing into all areas of education,' says Jarrod. While his first app was built using a web platform called Appmakr he soon had to outsource the more complicated apps with overseas programmers. He now works closely with a developer in the Ukraine. 'It's been a great relationship. He handles the heavy lifting, is paid for his services, and as a result is now able to afford a university education and travel.'

The PE Geek blog and website soon attracted a large worldwide following. Jarrod started travelling the world every school holiday break conducting workshops. Balancing his love of teaching, the growing demands of his business, and his own health and fitness became a challenge. In early 2015 Jarrod decided to take leave from his teaching position and restructure and grow the business to an entirely new level under his new company, ConnectedPE.

Most importantly, there have been significant changes as to how he does business. Jarrod now works on the 80/20 principle, focusing on the workshops, training and professional development for teachers. A six-month world tour took him to 10 countries focusing on the workshops. With the assistance of partner Amy, who also left her job so she can travel with him, Jarrod planned a successful global conference held in Dubai in October 2016. Over 150 educators attended from 15 countries.

From a #nolife hashtag Jarrod is now working fewer hours for more return by focusing on what he does best and outsourcing all other tasks, even the ones he is capable of doing himself, to freelance professionals. Essentially, he has tapped into a global talent pool. 'I use sites like upwork.com or ask other entrepreneurs for referrals,' he explains. 'For example, I can send them the raw audio footage and they can do the editing for my podcast.'

Essential for every business to grow, his all-important marketing is also outsourced and Jarrod pulls out his smart phone to demonstrate how a Slack tool can distribute work through multiple channels to various team members.

Instead of working harder to get more clients, Jarrod has embraced the philosophy of reverse marketing. 'Ninety per cent of our content is free,' he explains. 'We put content out through the newsletter, podcast, blog and social media explaining what we do and ultimately drawing clients to us whether it is a workshop or the mentoring program. Social media is the key.' Keeping his audience engaged and building an ongoing relationship is an important part of his strategy. 'I know who my customers are, where they live, and what they like.'

Back in Central Victoria for a break between engagements, Jarrod is clearly excited about what is happening in the technical world. 'We're seeing the start of a big disruption,' he says. 'It's not about government creating change, it is up to us.' He believes technology will have a much bigger role in the coming years. 'Artificial intelligence is currently seen as a gimmick but when developed further it will have a massive impact in the classroom.'

In case you haven't worked it out by now, Jarrod doesn't consider himself to be a traditional teacher. 'I don't do chalk, it's not my style.' He prefers encouraging students in active learning and self-discovery. In the privileged position of being able to observe changes in education on a global scale, Jarrod is at the cutting edge of education. 'Teachers think that content delivery is the most important but it's not. We're best at developing relationships and creating a learning environment for students.' According to Jarrod, transferring to working with students to adults hasn't been all that difficult. 'It's easy to work on a core idea with adults, you just have to be aware of the learning intent in the room.'

Viewing online videos of Jarrod's presentations and listening to his podcasts it becomes evident how he engages so well with his audiences.

Utilising his love of physical interaction with a passion for technology and new ideas, he is keen to share his knowledge. In 2020, his podcasts and online conferences feature guest speakers from all over the world. How apt for teachers who have been forced to adapt to remote teaching during the coronavirus restrictions!

A typical day for Jarrod is spent working online from his home office. Despite operating a global business, this use of online technology allows Jarrod to prioritise family and personal fitness. 'We certainly spend a lot of time meeting up with people across the planet,' Jarrod says. 'The offline ConnectedPE conference is now the world's largest event for PE teachers and is running right now with thousands of PE teachers from across the globe.'

JARROD'S TOP 5 BUSINESS TIPS:

- Turn off all your bad projects and focus on what you're best at.
- Outsource the tasks that others can do for you.
- Identify your good customers and work with them.
- Look for leveraged solutions to get more value.
- Consider automated and segmented systems to be more efficient.

  www.connectedpe.com

  www.thepegeek.com

Wholebrain

Wholebrain's principal teacher Janeen Barker and founder Denise Smith

Read an entrepreneur's biography and often you will find scathing references to their education, ranging from 'I couldn't wait to leave' to 'I was expelled'. It must be a huge surprise that these students, referred to by educators in hushed tones as 'disengaged', can go on to become successful businesspeople. Like Richard Branson, they aren't stupid; they just learn differently.

Imagine my delight when I chanced upon Wholebrain in Central Victoria, a program dedicated to inspiring disengaged students to learn. Wholebrain founder Denise Smith knows firsthand what it's like to be a right-brain learner in a left-brain-orientated education system. She experienced the difficulty of learning, as did her son. 'It tends to run in families regardless of gender,' she explains. 'We struggle with reading and become overwhelmed by everything in a normal classroom environment. Your self-esteem can suffer terribly.'

Dedicated to equipping students with right-brain learning tendencies to learn in a left-brain education system, Denise and her husband have donated a rural property at South Mandurang, just outside Bendigo, to host the program that primary school-aged students can attend one day a week. Classes for up to eight students are held in a non-threatening home environment while outdoor areas and a large shed host a range of physical activities, allowing students to learn by doing – which is their preference. The program is funded by parent fees and the occasional – and much appreciated – philanthropic donations.

'We want children to understand that they're not stupid, they just learn differently, and give them the tools to cope in their normal school environment,' explains Denise. 'We support the parents and teachers as well, helping them to understand the strengths of right-brain learners.'

Incredibly, Denise has spent over a decade developing a specific font, phonics program and word lists to help young people with dyslexia to cope in the classroom. Teachers immediately notice a difference when students are back in the normal classroom.

Janeen Barker has taken on the role of principal teacher at Wholebrain for the past 10 years. She is a fan of the program and, like Denise, Janeen has firsthand knowledge of right-brain learning – although it was not evident to her as a child. Growing up, Janeen never knew that her father could barely read, let alone write. How could she when he was such an active community leader and executive on so many different committees? What Janeen didn't know was that her mother was quietly helping in the background, writing the meeting minutes while he stuck to what he was good at, numbers. 'Dad always used to say there is more than one way to skin a cat,' Janeen recalls.

Occasionally he hit an obstacle, for instance when getting assessed to become an umpire for bowls. Despite getting 100% in the practical assessment, he failed the theory exam three times. 'Because Dad had a purpose to his learning he taught himself to pass the exam,' Janeen says with pride.

All this is painfully obvious to Janeen in retrospect, and she considers herself privileged to be a part of Wholebrain and able to make a real difference in the lives of future generations. 'We are giving these children life skills just as much as we are helping them at school,' Janeen observes. 'It's all about rediscovering the joy in learning.' How could you not enjoy learning at Wholebrain with such commitment and understanding, not to mention kangaroos grazing in and around your classroom?

As Wholebrain enters its 11th year of operation, students are entering the workforce and finding success. By understanding 'right *bright* learning' they are being put on the right track.

www.wholebrainworkout.com

Innovative

In a rapidly changing and highly competitive world with new challenges constantly on the horizon, every business must innovate. So many new products and services are just waiting to be created to meet new markets, but innovation does require patience and investment, with no guarantee of a return.

I am also constantly reminded that small innovations can have a major impact on the profitability and viability of rural businesses. Just look at how we do business and the way it has changed in recent decades and even more so in recent months under coronavirus restrictions. We are close to being a cashless society and automation is making data collection and analysis so much easier. When I recently rang a rice grower he was in the paddock where he'd just downloaded some data from his tractor to email through to his agronomist. Businesses are now drop-shipping orders to customers direct from the manufacturer without need for additional transport and storage.

No one can afford to be complacent in a highly competitive and global environment. We need to constantly review whether our products and services are still relevant, as well as the way we present and deliver them. Those that ignore technological advances risk being left behind. Even those small ideas such as a simple rebranding process can bring new markets and opportunities.

'So far we've developed the system from our own pockets with zero return.'

While our city counterparts enjoy access to the National Broadband Network, a solar-powered broadband repeating system and on-farm security sensor products developed by AgCloud in Central Victoria are assisting rural agricultural businesses to utilise technology.

'Innovation is achievable for everyone. It can be as simple as reinventing what's already out there or creating new packaging for your product to make it easier for your customers to use.'

A consummate marketer and innovator, Sarah Rose Bloom, co-founder of Simply Rose Petals, has constantly utilised technology to innovate and keep her business ahead of the many competitors that subsequently scrambled in her footsteps.

'Every Sunday I used to give kilos and kilos of lamb bellies to my neighbours to feed their kelpies.'

Toni Barton, a Central Victorian lamb farmer, has had to educate regulators that it is possible to innovate and that not all bacon has to be made from pork.

'We all knew I had a winner and didn't want to let a great idea go to waste.'

Charlie Webb in the Riverina region of New South Wales decided to delve into the psychology of sheep so that his life as a farmer, and that of his woolly charges, are made easier. After months of tinkering and testing, the result was Back Up Charlie, an award-winning flexible sheep movement system.

'We had to have an agile mindset as we were constantly and deliberately building in feedback loops to learn from customers.'

It has been fascinating following the journey of Localised, a start-up based in regional Victoria that has created an online social network for local business to solve an important problem.

Happy innovating!

AgCloud

Grant Sutton, AgCloud

As we often say out in the bush, there is more than one way to skin a cat. Having never personally done so I repeat this at face value, but I can testify as to how innovative rural people are when it comes to problem solving. Such is the case when it comes to the National Broadband Network (NBN) and the inequitable service being presented to rural Australia.

In spring 2017, amid the green rolling hills of Central Victoria, a group of farmers was given a sneak preview of a solar-powered broadband repeating system that allowed a daisy-chain radio network to be realised. The prototype had been developed by a Bendigo-based start-up, aptly named AgCloud.

Showcasing his new purpose-built shearing shed and workshop, fourth generation stud merino breeder Jock MacRae set the scene by describing his frustration at not being able to utilise the full benefits of the NBN in his business. Empathising with Jock's frustration – and that of many other rural clients in similar circumstances – Grant Sutton, a self-employed IT professional from Big Hill near Bendigo, recognised the problem and, with the help of some colleagues, found a solution.

'Grant was able to help us connect to the NBN when most providers were saying it couldn't be done. Once connected to the residence, he was able to take it via a hilltop to the farm infrastructure a few kilometres down the road at Elphinstone,' explains Jock. 'This has delivered low-cost high-speed internet right across the farm. From operations in the sheep yards and cattle yards, the workshop and shearing shed, right down to the monitoring of an individual animal, this is the solution I had been looking for.'

Grant says that Jock's case is just one of many. 'Neighbours separated by a single hill are finding that one is eligible for high-speed internet services while the other is relegated to either congested Next-G or slow and expensive satellite services,' explains Grant. 'Our aim has been to address the inequality by repeating services over hills and terrain to fill that void in the service difference. By linking high-speed NBN we're exploring what high-quality internet can do for them.'

In the case of the prototype service established at Jock's property, the benefits are already significant, particularly in the area of farm security and NBN provision. 'We've installed fixed cameras and gate tags at key points around the property and I can now access live data and receive alerts via my smart phone,' says a clearly delighted Jock, who is ever conscious of protecting and monitoring his assets. All this has been achieved by simply installing a repeating service at the highest point of the property, something I overlooked when driving in but paid special attention to on the drive out. Solar panels overcome remote power issues and there is the potential to also install wind turbines to ensure continuity in the winter months.

But what happens if the connection is broken or equipment tampered with, I wonder? 'Notifications are immediately received by the client,' responds Grant, whose expert team has considered the process carefully. 'Farm-sensing products are also solar powered and can be used for a vast number of sensing requirements,' he adds. 'Anything from silo levels, livestock locations and environmental conditions can be recorded into the cloud and understood by the farmer from anywhere in the world.'

For farmers who have large remote properties and like to take time off with their families, this is particularly good news. From Jock's perspective he will be able to check live feed and respond to alerts from wherever he might be.

Having collaborated with electronic specialists, programmers, and manufacturers, Grant has successfully developed a prototype service and products that surpass any off-the-shelf hardware currently available on the market.

Capital funding then became AgCloud's next challenge. 'So far we've developed the system from our own pockets with zero return,' says Grant, who is sincerely grateful to the local individuals and businesses that have

Duncan Barber, a Central Victorian farmer and parent of four children, expressing his delight with his new NBN repeater station.

generously given their time and resources to get the prototype to this point. 'We are now looking for some serious funding to take us to the next level and roll this service out Australia wide and potentially to a global market.'

He is chuffed when we catch up for a chat in February 2020. AgCloud's recently launched security sensor has just been featured in the *Weekly Times* providing the business with some great publicity. The sensor is being utilised to address a series of ongoing thefts in a community of small rural properties. 'It's a bit like Neighbourhood Watch but with technology,' Grant explains. 'The sensor can direct a SMS alert to a neighbour when they are away from home and someone enters their property perimeter. The technology can also turn on a television or light to imply that someone is home, effectively deterring intruders.'

Since we last spoke AgCloud has branched out into two main areas: farm connectivity and network management, as well as its suite of farm security products. While they didn't receive the much hoped-for funding assistance for their repeater system prototype, AgCloud and its flagship product has continued to grow. 'We've engaged with some massive farms and rural industries such as Hazeldines since that initial trial.'

Having just had three products accepted in the Victorian Government's On-Farm Internet of Things trial, Grant says they're currently gearing up to meet the anticipated demand from farmers across the State. 'This could be a game changer,' he says.

And then came COVID-19. With some trepidation I contact him in May 2020 to ask how it has affected business. 'Business is booming,' he tells me with a big smile. With children being home schooled it appears that farmers are using up all their data and discovering that they can't cope on satellite. 'We've sold more repeater stations the last couple of months than previously. We've received orders from everywhere including a cattle station in Queensland and a piggery in New South Wales.'

In addition, AgCloud has commenced an official pilot of their system with NBN Co. 'NBN Co are putting it through the wringer and writing the rules for this solution for all of Australia.'

Just goes to show that innovation thrives in a pandemic!

www.agcloud.com.au

Simply Rose Petals

Sarah Rose Bloom, Simply Roses (photo supplied)

When Sarah Rose Bloom helped reinvent her mother's farm of 1000 rose plants in 2004, no one in the cut-flower industry could have foreseen just how much this new business would innovate and bloom.

Spurred on by her inability to get a job with a career focus upon returning to her hometown of Swan Hill, Sarah put her science degree and entrepreneurial spirit to good use researching alternatives to a struggling cut-flower industry. 'At this time traditional confetti started being frowned upon at wedding venues because it caused staining and was not biodegradable,' explains Sarah. 'We saw an opportunity and went for it.'

Simply Rose Petals was subsequently launched on an unsuspecting public by this dynamic mother–daughter duo. And when I say launched, I mean it in every possible way, including confetti cannons that shoot the petals up to four metres high and the product being featured on popular Australian television shows such as *The Bachelor, X Factor, Dancing With The Stars, The Bachelorette* and *Big Brother*!

Sarah has constantly utilised technology to keep Simply Rose Petals ahead of the following pack. Specialised technology allows their rose petals to be freeze-dried, packaged and shipped to 15 countries around the world. Such has been the demand that they have expanded their number of rose plants from 1000 to 6000.

From her rural office surrounded by roses on the banks of the mighty Murray River, Sarah spends thousands of hours online each year researching ideas to ensure the business progresses. Social media has played a major factor. Scholarships and awards have also been useful tools. In 2006 she received a Churchill Fellowship to travel to 11 countries exploring effective processing, packaging and storage techniques, and the latest mechanisation trends in the flower industry. With harvesting of rose petals the most labour-intensive activity, Sarah had hoped to discover a way of mechanising this process during her Fellowship.

'Unfortunately, I was unable to discover a machine capable of removing the petals without damaging or bruising them,' she says. She was, however, able to analyse the latest in air-drying versus freeze-drying technology. She continued to search for more knowledge. Through a Nuffield Scholarship in 2014 Sarah explored further uses for rose petals, including edible and organic rose petals in a growing 'foodie' culture, spurred on by cooking shows such as *MasterChef*. 'Despite food certification challenges in Australia, the Nuffield tour convinced me that rose petals can be successfully produced organically and there is plenty of scope for creating specialty foods and nutritional supplements derived from rose petals,' says Sarah.

With an insatiable curiosity and boundless enthusiasm driving her to improve the business, it is no surprise that Sarah has been recognised as a finalist through the Telstra Businesswomen's Awards and, in 2015, received the Veuve Clicquot New Generation Award for female Australian entrepreneur under 40.

In 2018 co-owners Sarah Rose Bloom and Jan Slater were named in the Top 50 Small Business Leaders in Australia, won the National Bridal Industry Award for Unique Services, and the Victorian Regional and Communities Award for Agricultural Innovation. In 2019 Simply Rose Petals was inducted into Australian Bridal Industry Hall of Fame.

Make no mistake. Constantly exploring opportunities to introduce new products, methods and technologies has been an integral part of this enterprising rural businesswoman's journey. It has also helped the business to survive during the coronavirus restrictions and their impact on weddings. After the flurry of Valentine's Day, Sarah has focused marketing on their edible rose petals. Instagram photos show off a range of beautiful cakes and dishes.

Simply Rose Petals is still blooming on the banks of the mighty Murray!

SARAH'S TOP BUSINESS TIPS:

- Every business requires a determination and persistence that can only be fuelled by passion and hard work. Make sure you are in it for the long haul, not short financial gain.
- Innovation can be as simple as reinventing what's already out there or creating new packaging for your product that makes it easier for your customers to use.
- You can't expect your business to be healthy if you don't take care of yourself first. The health, fitness and mental wellbeing of the entrepreneur is crucial.

www.simplyrosepetals.com.au

Lamb Bacon

Toni Barton, Barton's Smallgoods (photo supplied)

Nulla Vale lamb farmer and enterprising creator of Lamb Bacon, Toni Barton displays all the attributes of a typical entrepreneur. Some would say she is driven. Ideas are explored, problems solved, and opportunities taken. At the core of it all is Toni's deliberate life-choice, to trade in an international marketing career for that of a hands-on farmer producing good quality meat.

Mondays aren't Toni's favourite day. She has a load of lambs to deliver to the abattoir. She undertakes this task each week. 'I take animal welfare seriously and have developed a good relationship with the abattoir in Kyneton,' she explains. 'Hardwicks are very good in supporting small producers.'

Another day she didn't enjoy was discovering 20 dead and injured sheep in the paddock following a dog attack. 'It was one of the most traumatic experiences of my life,' she says. Welcome to the life of a farmer.

After a lot of soul searching, in 2016 Toni gave up her international lifestyle in corporate marketing to reinvent herself as a farmer. In preparation for the transition, she had purchased 60 hectares of prime grazing land at Nulla Vale near Lancefield and converted three big paddocks into 15 smaller ones for rotational grazing. She set it up as a three-tiered business: breeding and selling Australian White stud rams, producing lambs, and selling lamb meat products.

In her first year she processed 16 lambs for meat, which was sold to family and friends. The following year it was 30 lambs. Four years on as a full-time farmer, she is processing 600 lambs annually with a profit of over $200 per lamb sold through customer-centric distribution channels, including online and farmers' markets. Such has the demand grown for her meat that she is now collaborating with four select sheep farmers who have taken on her breeding rams and share the same farming ethics of grass fed and animal husbandry. 'One hundred per cent grass fed and no chemicals,' Toni explains. As a result, she has regular cutting and mulching of the paddocks on her long list of chores. She also makes a point of paying premium prices to her fellow farmers so they can maintain their sustainable farming practices and avoid the pressures of mass production and grain feeding regimes.

But it was her creation of the iconic Lamb Bacon in 2016 that really put Toni in the public eye, drawing scrutiny from the Prime Safe authority. Lamb Bacon was created in response to Toni's annoyance over the lamb bellies not being used. 'Every Sunday I used to give kilos and kilos of lamb bellies to my neighbours to feed to their kelpies.'

On long road trips she would constantly challenge her brain to think of something new. And she did. Who would have thought that bacon could be made from anything but pork? Experiments with her American friend and *BBQ Pitmaster* Jon meant that she could road test flavour profiles and cooking techniques. 'As soon as I tasted it, I knew I was on to something,' Toni smiles. Samples were shared with regular customers and high-profile chefs readily endorsed it as a great alternative to traditional bacon made from pork bellies.

Toni fully understood her obligations of food safety and microbiological testing to ensure her duty of care to consumers, but with a new innovative product hitting the market there are many negative attitudes encountered. 'If I had a dollar for the number of times I've heard: You can't do that!'

Top of the hurdle list would have to be a sudden directive from Prime Safe, which regulates Australia's meat industry, to immediately shut down production and recall all her Lamb Bacon products from sale. 'I just sat in the paddock in total disbelief,' Toni admits. She immediately rang her smokehouse instructing them to stop production but the ramifications of recalling hundreds of products already on supermarket shelves was catastrophic.

Moving into problem-solving mode, Toni fought back the emotion and focused on the process. Overnight she read through the *Food Standards Act* and researched the topic globally. She was able to determine that no one species, for example pork, was defined as bacon in Australia. In the early hours of the morning she sent a carefully composed email to Prime Safe outlining her findings. Much to her relief, a phone call from Prime Safe a few hours later announced a reversal of their decision and Toni was congratulated on her initiative.

A big part of Toni's role has been to educate regulators that it is possible to innovate. 'I made sure that alternate bacon options were approved by Prime Safe for the benefit of other future products, including duck bacon and beef bacon.' She also ensured that the Australian Meat Industry Council was made aware of the findings. 'This is the challenge of food innovation, you are constantly fighting an uphill battle to get the product accepted by industry and regulators.'

Transferring her skills to farming and food production has required considerable research on other fronts. An intensive 14-week accelerator program enabled her to become more strategic. As part of her start-up process she set up an advisory board of skilled and experienced professionals to offer her valuable guidance. Her marketing skills allowed her to set up a website to sell direct to the public and social media to publicise her products. Recruiting quality staff and paying attention to detail have also been crucial. 'People buy with their eyes, so all my products need to be well presented, from the labelling to the pricing. Customers need certainty and it takes at least a year and lots of investment to develop a business and brand profile. You don't plan to be an entrepreneur,' she reflects. 'I feel like everything I've done in my life has brought me to this moment.'

Toni admits that it can be lonely at times, but so far she has resisted taking on a business partner or a commercial loan. Her number-one supporter until her death in 2018 was her mum. She is particularly grateful to her dad who is called upon to do important jobs around the farm and neighbours who are always willing to help out.

While the world has been more recently reeling from the shock of COVID-19, on the farm it has been business as usual for Toni. 'Jobs still have to be done.' Through the farmers' markets and her online delivery service (both classified as an essential service) Toni is very much aware of the impact. Protecting her carefully established ecosystem has been a top priority.

'Supply is critical,' Toni observes. 'When it's convenient consumers go to the supermarkets, but when there is a threat they go direct to the source. At the farmers' market at Flemington, I had to convince customers not to panic buy and reassure them that I would be there the following week,' she explained. While increasing her sales slightly in response, she is very aware that this also places pressure on her to source more sheep that meet her criteria, as well as on her butcher to process the meat. 'Hats off to the farmers' market organisers,' Toni adds. 'They have become experts in crowd control, social distancing and hygiene. This is above and beyond their job description.'

Looking after regular customers has been another priority. Toni was stunned to discover how many of her customers have compromised immune systems, keeping them in self-isolation at home. Her online sales platform has provided the opportunity for customers to pre-order and pay to reduce the time to wait in long lines at the markets, and also enable her to make home deliveries.

'Three days a week I get up at 4 am to attend farmers' markets and then I do customer deliveries around the bayside area afterwards, getting home at seven at night.'

Her days are long and there are multiple decisions to be made, but Toni is living where she most loves to be. 'This is why I started and where I want to stay. I want to grow food and give people access to good quality meat.'

www.mikonipark.com.au

Back Up Charlie

Charlie Webb, Back Up Charlie

Whether it is fair or not, sheep are often referred to in derogatory terms when it comes to their intelligence; usually when they break away from the mob and make the lives of their handlers a misery. Charlie Webb decided to delve into the psychology of sheep so that his life as a farmer, and his woolly charges, is made much easier. The result is Back Up Charlie.

When Back Up Charlie, a flexible lead-up race for sheep handlers, was awarded Machine of the Year at the Henty Field Days in 2016, Charlie Webb felt very satisfied. He already knew that it was a winner because he'd invented it for use on his farm. The public recognition made his task of marketing this new innovation to other farmers all the easier. A subsequent award at Orange in 2017 confirmed that Back Up Charlie was on the road to success.

To hear more about this award-winning innovation, I caught up with Charlie Webb at his lakeside property just outside Lockhart in New South Wales, on the day of his eldest daughter Phillippa's wedding in October 2018. What was usually a working shearing shed had been transformed into a reception venue for the guests shortly due to arrive. A quick tour confirmed that I was talking to a man who likes to make things with his own hands and do them well. Charlie had constructed a bar especially for the wedding and a tour of the shearing quarters revealed five-star luxury in terms of this traditionally rough-and-ready industry. Contrary to my previous experiences in shearing sheds, I had no qualms about accepting a cup of coffee, with milk, from the spotless kitchenette as we settled down for a chat.

It was a classic case of problem solving. Charlie wanted to move his sheep more effectively from the holding yard into automated sheep handlers, crutching plants and other sheep-handling applications. No other systems he had tried seemed to work, no matter how much was invested.

'I designed Back Up Charlie for myself,' he says. 'It was about making our job easier. It's faster, cuts down on labour and is kinder on the sheep. We used to be exhausted pushing sheep in the yards from 7 am until 6 pm. I knew it worked the day I was able to knock off at 4.30 pm and go home to help Tana (his wife) in the garden.'

It was 2015 when Charlie disappeared into his shed over a period of four months to develop a prototype. 'Tana asked what in the hell I'd been doing,' he recalls with a grin. Materials were challenging to source, and it was a matter of trial and error. A welding course at college and over 40 years' experience of sheep farming were put to good use. There was also a lot of thinking. 'It was very much about animal psychology and how sheep react in stressful situations,' he explains.

Having discussed the inadequacy of previous systems with a livestock contractor friend, Charlie was quick to get on the phone to share the news. 'He came down with a group to watch me demonstrate it and they didn't say anything for a whole 10 minutes,' Charlie recalls. 'We all knew I had a winner and didn't want to let a great idea go to waste.'

With the help of another daughter, Josephine, who has a Bachelor of Business in Agriculture and is actively working on the farm, Charlie started the process of setting up a business to market and sell the new system, now branded Back Up Charlie. He already had a good accountant and sourced marketing expertise. Agreeing on the right wording and images proved a challenge. As a farmer himself, Charlie had no illusions. 'Selling product to farmers is a tough task!'

His other priority was to manufacture the units locally. 'You have to share your success with the locals,' he says. 'You can't beat people down on price in a small town like Lockhart.' Mark Schirmer, a local engineer, readily agreed and they were off and manufacturing. 'We set our pricing based on the materials and the 70+ man-hours it takes to make a unit,' Charlie explains.

Three years in the making and Back Up Charlie is established. 'It's been a process to get it out to the market. There is no point spending big dollars on something that doesn't do the job – which has been the case with so many other systems I've looked at over the years.'

The Henty and Orange Field Day Awards provided much needed publicity. 'It was free advertising and helped to get the Back Up Charlie branding into people's heads,' Charlie says. 'Over two years we've sold 30 units in New South Wales and across the borders into Victoria and South Australia.' Josephine updates Facebook and Instagram pages, helping promote the brand.

When I ask Charlie about what he recommends to others who have invented a new product, he quickly responds: 'Make sure you have a unique product and protect your idea.' This includes applying patents if required. When it comes to finding experienced support, Charlie adds that you should always ask other experienced business people for recommendations and keep going until you find the right ones to work with. They have to understand you and your business.

With the arrival of the crucial bridegroom and his family, heralded by plumes of dust along the driveway through the paddocks, I realise my time is up with this talented backyard inventor and sheep psychologist. I am extremely grateful to have heard another great rural business story.

Charlie reports in 2020 that he's had a very quiet year, due to the drought rather than coronavirus. 'We are still getting a lot of enquiries though,' he adds, 'people just need to recover mentally and financially from the drought before they can think ahead.' Not one to sit around, he lets slip that they are looking to introduce another business idea. 'We are just sorting out a few things so we can do a full cost analysis before proceeding,' he tells me.

Can't wait to see what he next comes up with!

CHARLIE'S TOP BUSINESS TIPS:

- Make sure your idea and product is unique.
- Get recommendations from experienced businesspeople.
- Ensure there is a market for your idea or product.
- Protect your idea and product.
- Follow your dreams.

www.backupcharlie.com.au

Localised

Theo Williams, Localised

With an increasing number of remote workers and home-based businesses operating in rural and regional areas, it is not surprising how little we know about who is operating in our own backyard. A regional entrepreneur set out to solve this problem in 2016 and I've been fortunate to follow the journey of Localised, an online social network for local business, over the past four years. It is perfectly placed to meet an urgent need in 2020.

I first met with Theo Williams in 2017 over a coffee. Theo explained that he and a friend, James Baird, became start-up founders. After a year of working on the problem of local business discovery, Theo had the task of marketing a new digital platform and tool to the local government sector. I was fascinated to learn that neither James nor Theo had any technical expertise in designing software; they engaged a Gippsland-based development agency for that task. What the pair did have was the vision and passion to drive the idea of connecting local business.

Initially investors were sought to get the company started and the Geelong Angel Investors Network enabled Localised to get off the ground. 'I came in with sweat equity,' Theo admits. 'We both paid ourselves crap wages for a year as we worked to get the business going. It seemed like we were forever in the experimental stage,' he recalls. 'We had to have an agile mindset as we were constantly and deliberately building in feedback loops to learn from customers.'

The timing was right. The historical manufacturing centre of Geelong was taking off as it reinvented itself as a place of start-ups and entrepreneurs. Localised found support and inspiration through fellow start-up organisations like Runway.

A second version of the digital platform, launched in early 2017, continues to be incrementally improved. Theo's task was to market the product to councils as a low-cost digital tool to assist local businesses to connect. As the promotional literature explains: *Localised is an online place-based network for local business. Helping businesses find local providers of products and services, share business advice and news with each other, and to connect to business events and local clients.*

'Local is subjective,' explains Theo. 'It could be a small town in the USA or the Wimmera. Localised is a social network for businesses similar to LinkedIn for professional people.' The platform he could find most like Localised was Town Square in the USA, but nothing directly connected people in business. 'We had to make a lot of noise, including cold calling and getting brand exposure through sponsorship at industry events attended by economic development professionals.'

Enterprise Geelong jumped on board early as a platform partner, as did other rural-based councils. From late 2019, metropolitan councils started showing interest and the customer base expanded Australia wide. Councils purchase an annual data licence, which gives them access to rich data about local businesses. Quarterly reports provide updates and the platform is designed to help businesses promote themselves to a local market.

A big selling point for Localised has been the growth in home-based businesses that often have zero visibility in a community. 'It's hard to measure the impact of business-to-business activity,' admits Theo, 'but we do have lots of anecdotal evidence. In the gig economy, counting full-time equivalent (FTE) jobs is an archaic way of measuring economic development.' Once councils are signed up, social media, direct mail and flyers included with rates notices are essential in making businesses aware of the Localised platform.

An early lesson for Theo was that a digital platform was not enough. 'Businesspeople also want to meet face to face so we developed commercially focused, yet fun, business networking events as well.' This also serves as an ideal marketing opportunity for those businesses yet to build digital literacy.

James Baird (left) at an event with fellow team members

Another interesting aspect about Localised is that a remote worker model works well for the company itself. The three key staff members live across regional Victoria.

'Google Hangouts and phone is how we work. Short, sharp catch-ups every morning. We work in and around kinder drop-offs,' says Theo. While use of technology is part of their everyday work, he admits that there are some challenges within the local government sector with staff sometimes struggling to video conference and electing to bring in their own laptops to communicate with the Localised team.

Over a series of coffees and phone chats, Theo and I touched base in mid-2019 and again in January 2020 when he announces his appointment as Chief Executive Officer and advises that James is working on a new start-up venture. 'We had two totally different products targeting different markets, so we decided to split the business. This way James can focus on developing the new intellectual property and I can focus totally on Localised,' Theo explains. 'We still work closely and support each other where we can.'

Having advanced significantly from securing their first sign-up, the Localised platform is now operating across 38 councils and has in excess of 6000 business members. There are 547 councils Australia wide and Theo is aiming to partner with at least 200. Given a sudden uptake in business development during COVID-19 one can expect that this goal is becoming closer. 'A digital community is now seen as a legitimate way of connecting,' he reaffirms.

Given all the development over the past four years, you could be tempted to say that Localised has hit that 'sweet spot' in terms of meeting client needs, but Theo is far from complacent. 'It's been business as usual for us during COVID-19. We've introduced a new jobs platform and are building a capability register for enterprise sales. Technology drives change but also has to react to change,' he cautions. Can't wait for our next coffee catch-up!

www.localised.com.au

Opportunistic

Not everyone who sees an open door will walk through it. Grabbing an opportunity requires courage and determination and I can think of no better example than these four incredible businesses.

'If I think of a good idea, I just run with it.'

For Lauren Mathers it all started when she had the problem of sourcing local pork for her restaurant. When Lauren embarked on a business journey with Doris the Berkshire sow she identified even more obstacles. She strategically chose to approach these problems as opportunities.

'You don't plan to be an entrepreneur. I feel like everything I've done in my life has brought me to this moment.'

Despite the complexity of exporting, Toni Barton has discovered the benefits of being an Australian lamb producer and manufacturer. Provenance is very important in the export market and Australian meat is highly regarded. In addition, no one else is exporting processed lamb products. Buyers at Gulfood in Dubai were amazed to learn that Toni was the actual sheep farmer. 'I was made to feel like a celebrity,' she told me as she was preparing to return to the Middle East for a publicity photo shoot.

'I wanted to make my own decisions, become my own boss.'

Brendan Earl, a young Indigenous plumber in Western Australia, noticed that clean treated water was becoming a commodity. People becoming increasingly health conscious meant a demand for water filtration – and Calybre Plumbing & Gas was transformed to Keip Filtration to meet the need.

'We had similar ideas about how we could help grow a secondary economy in Sea Lake and all got quite passionate about this project.'

When tourists started arriving in their droves to view the acclaimed Lake Tyrrell mirror images at sunset, Ross Williams saw an opportunity to fill a gap in the accommodation market and benefit his agricultural hometown.

Bundarra Berkshires

Lauren Mathers, Bundarra Berkshires

Lauren Mathers gave birth to three children in the midst of becoming a free-range farmer and exemplifying the paddock to plate dream. Displaying the attributes of a true entrepreneur, she started Bundarra Berkshires when she saw a problem that could be turned into an opportunity. And history keeps repeating itself.

Arriving at the Mathers property near Barham in New South Wales early one brisk mid-winter morning in 2018, it comes as no surprise that bacon and eggs are on the menu. The kids are sleeping in and Lachlan and Lauren are planning their weekend ahead. No football. No socialising. Weekends are the best time for the couple to do the hands-on work required to care for their 400-plus Berkshire pigs.

'It was madness when I look back. I used to do it all, but Lachlan stepped in and shared the responsibilities as the children came along,' explains Lauren. A transport driver for his parents' company during the week, Lachlan has been pleasantly surprised at how enjoyable it has been to get involved in a business that is now their main source of income. 'I'm trucks by day and pigs by night and weekends,' he smiles. 'Dad and husband is in there somewhere as well.' All jokes aside, he adds he is enjoying his new role. 'Lachlan is a great salesman and loves chatting with the customers and fellow stallholders,' Lauren chips in. 'Until he started coming to the markets with me, he'd never seen that side of the business.'

With our plates empty I chat with Lauren over coffee as Lachlan deals with the waking kids. It quickly becomes apparent how her brain operates. Constantly. Very fast. And, no doubt, she is a problem-solver. 'If I think of a good idea I just run with it,' she admits.

OPPORTUNITY #1 Sourcing local quality pork

Lauren had her first experience of small business as a partner in the successful The Long Paddock restaurant established in 2008 at nearby Koondrook on the Victorian side of the Murray River. The restaurant's reputation was built on an ethos of sourcing local quality foods, but she was having trouble finding tasty pork. This is how Doris first came on the scene.

'A bloke down the road had a Berkshire pig that he didn't want any more,' Lauren explains, 'so I reckoned I would have a go at breeding my own pork.' Being raised on a beef cattle farm was of no use whatsoever when it came to collecting the founding member of her breeding stock. With the owner absent Lauren tried to herd the pig – later named Doris – on to the trailer. 'She was like a wild dog,' Lauren recalls. 'My first lesson was in how to bribe pigs with food and make it a positive experience.'

While Doris failed to produce a litter for some time, ironically Lauren fell pregnant with her first child. Undeterred, the seed of an idea just grew and grew, fuelled by a bursary as a Rural Ambassador to visit France and see how farmers there sold their produce at markets and study the relationship between consumer and farmer.

Eight years since establishing the herd, Lauren now has to care for over 100 sows and 300 piglets at any given time. And, for those of you who are wondering, Doris lived on despite her shortcomings, eventually dying from natural causes.

OPPORTUNITY #2 Finding customers

'It was clear when I came back from my trip to France that we needed a local market, so I helped set up the Red Gum Group and Farmers' Market,' Lauren explains. 'Now there are lots of farmers' markets, which everyone loves. Until recently we regularly attended the Melbourne markets and will continue to attend the Castlemaine market each month and possibly get back into Melbourne once a month now that Mum and Dad are here to help out.'

By late 2011 Lauren was selling gourmet pork products to retail outlets and at farmers' markets. 'Winning a Delicious Product Award in 2013 was a great kick start,' she acknowledges.

Bundarra Berkshires has its own website and Farm Shop page outlining products that can either be purchased at one of the listed stockists or delivered through their courier service. Hogfest, held each September, promotes the 'paddock to plate' concept and connects customers with their products. Social media has clearly been a winner with a healthy following on Facebook and Instagram. Quality photography assists Lauren to clearly articulate a love of animals and a rural family lifestyle.

'There are now a lot more micro businesses operating in this field,' Lauren admits, 'so we have to work hard to stay ahead of the game. Over the past two years we have been constantly tweaking our targets. Clean eating means nitrate free and preservative free so we concentrate our energy here. You have to pick an area and own it,' she advises.

OPPORTUNITY #3 Controlling supply

While many businesses are transitioning to a lean balance sheet through outsourcing, Lauren believes that agriculture is moving in the opposite direction, especially when it comes to clean, green, and ethically produced food. 'There is too much uncertainty if we don't,' she explains.

Keen to know her business every step of the way, she started by helping her preferred butcher at Gunbower to pack her pork products. 'Tom showed me all the different parts and how to bone out a shoulder. Lucy, our eldest child, was in a pram at the time,' she recalls. Soon the logistics of taking Lucy to the butcher and struggling to find other butchers to do smoking and sausages for her became stressful and time consuming. Just as their second child, Frida, was born in 2013, Lauren recognised what many would perceive to be a problem as an opportunity. 'I decided to take control of our own supply.' Subsequently the shed was cleaned out and a cutting room and smokehouse installed. A year after that a commercial kitchen and air-drying room was added.

Before you start thinking this is all too easy, finance did prove problematic for this second phase of the business, so Lauren tried out a Crowd Funding campaign by offering produce in return for advance payments to help fit out the new facilities. 'The campaign raised more than we aimed for, but I probably wouldn't do it again,' she admits.

To help get her started, a friend spent a day instructing Lauren on the different cuts for meat. 'For the first three years I butchered on my own with a handsaw which kept costs really low.' As the demand for product grew a butcher was employed in late 2015, perfect timing to assist with the Christmas rush and, by my calculations, to aid Lauren who was pregnant with George, child number three!

'To begin with we used what buildings we had but we are outgrowing ourselves now.' Another problem and/or opportunity for her to think about.

Lauren also feels passionate about humane slaughter of the pigs, especially in the current climate where many abattoirs are closing or denying access to micro producers. After a series of abattoir closures and an increase in road miles impacting on their transport costs of 10 pigs each week, Lauren is once again taking a lead in providing a solution. 'Ideally we'd like to slaughter 15 pigs a week, but the logistics are against us because of the truck size.'

In her latest quest, Lauren is part of a group of likeminded farmers in the process of establishing a local cooperative to set up their own micro abattoir. Her vision, shared by the group, is for it to be staffed with highly skilled personnel operating under an ethos of humane treatment of animals. 'Offal is another big opportunity to create new products from waste and, as a cooperative, we will also be able to put back into the community,' Lauren says with a sparkle in her eye.

Much to Lauren's frustration, problem #4 is still in the process of being turned into an opportunity as the effects of an impending drought start to make their mark. 'Usually we are knee deep in pasture this time of the year, but we've had no rain and we're at the mercy of a feed company. The price of feed has just gone up $100 per tonne.' Sourcing feed with no animal base has been a difficult process. There is no quick fix to this one, but I have no doubt that Lauren will keep thinking on it. Expanding their 26-hectare farm is one strategy, and she has already sub-contracted her parents on a nearby property to grow out pigs for her.

'I am a thinker,' Lauren acknowledges. 'The challenges are what I love. I strive to get it better and stay ahead. As a society we are still so disconnected from our food, but Bundarra Berkshires is pure paddock to plate. It's pretty amazing.' Winning #bestbrandedpork at the #AusFoodAwards in 2019 for the second time in three years confirms that others agree with her.

We catch up in February 2020 and Lauren fills me in on the rest of her exciting news. 'We're expanding this year! We've built a bigger butchery in Barham and attached a deli to it. We're doing coffee and take-home pork meals, plus all our products and other regional products that complement our products like wine, cheese, etc.'

Clearly, Lauren is most excited about the new packing facility, which is providing them with much-needed additional space and equipment. 'This is being export rated so we can send our products out fresh and value added into Singapore,' she adds.

'We're only doing one farmers' market a month now as our online pork box system is going really well and helped to replace our income from the markets. Our new deli will hopefully be a roaring success and keep us off the road!'

Well, those were fateful words because a few weeks later, coronavirus restrictions came into force. I was a little fearful for their new venture. 'We've been very lucky,' Lauren is quick to assure me. 'Local support has been wonderful, and it has been easy to adapt.'

In other news, Lauren was appointed chair of the Murray Plains Meat Cooperative in 2019, pursuing a dream of providing close-to-home and humane slaughtering facilities for small producers.

'The coop is going well, the abattoir has been taken on by the council, which is great! They have allocated drought funding to it and see it as a valuable asset for our region. The cooperative will lease to own the facility in five years, it's getting great traction now.'

With the dry conditions continuing Lauren is delighted that a local businessman has offered them the use of his farm to finish growing out their pigs. Sounds like they're on a roll.

LAUREN'S TOP BUSINESS TIPS:

- Have a clear vision of what you want to achieve and stick to it.
- At the same time, be aware of new opportunities to improve your business and be prepared to change and adapt.
- Don't do it if you don't love it.

  www.littleporkdeli.com.au

Barton's Smallgoods

Toni Barton, Barton's Smallgoods

Toni Barton of Lamb Bacon fame is back from exploring new export market opportunities in Dubai. What she thought would be a simple name change has turned into a full rebranding and a suite of new products destined for the Middle East. She is also discovering how complex and costly preparing for export can be when it comes to a highly regulated food industry. But the biggest surprise of all was the celebrity status thrust upon her for being an Australian lamb producer.

In February 2019 Toni travelled to Gulfood, the world's largest food conference held in Dubai. She was part of the Victorian Government's trade mission to explore the 'appetite' for her processed lamb products. Based on prior research, she had modest expectations for the four products on offer. But, as her fellow delegates headed off to the pub each night, Toni was still in discussions and writing up orders. Her projections quickly escalated. 'Provenance is very important in the export market and Australian meat has amazing equity. Middle Eastern countries love Australian lamb. My suite of products has been picked up by the five and six-star hotels and high-end supermarkets in Oman, Dubai, Qatar, and Kuwait,' she explained.

Thanks to the *Weekly Time*'s Shine Awards, Toni had grown accustomed to publicity in the months before, but nothing prepared her for the reaction in Dubai. 'Just because I'm a sheep farmer, I was made to feel like a celebrity. I've been totally overwhelmed by the response,' she admitted.

Prior to her visit Toni was already aware that her iconic Lamb Bacon brand was destined to remain on Australian soil. She had to clearly delineate her lamb products from pork in countries that adhere to strict Halal practices. A new name was required for export. Her initial plan was to simply change the name from Lamb Bacon to Lamb Rashers, but Tony felt it was still a bit dubious – and she had a suite of products to sell.

'In 48 hours, just before I took off for Dubai, I did a total rebrand, printed labels, and created a new website – Barton's Smallgoods – to avoid confusion. It was crazy.' But her marketing skills from a former corporate life came in handy. And thanks to a Meat Livestock Australia (MLA) producer-led innovation grant, Toni has received financial assistance to navigate her way through the export process. 'While there is a lot of information available through the government, no one else is exporting processed lamb products so this is totally new. My role is to learn how to streamline the process and share my knowledge with other producers,' she explained, urging anyone with similar products to contact her. 'I'm happy to answer questions.'

One by one Toni is dealing with multiple challenges to get her unique products export ready. She rattles off an extensive list of the licensing bodies to which she must submit paperwork, meet assessment, and pay fees. She estimates that it will require at least $100,000 before she produces a single product. 'While Australia already exports a lot of meat to the Middle East, it's a complex environment made very difficult for small producers,' she says. The engagement of HACCP and Export consultants has been a necessity during the process.

'My products are meat, it's processed meat, it's lamb, and they're brand-new products that haven't been done globally before. These all add layers of complexity. It isn't just about getting your facility export ready and ensuring that you are using accredited export logistic organisations,' cautions Toni. 'You also need to consider that each individual product has to be certified by the government to its export destination, as well as meeting Halal certification requirements.'

Toni has leased part of a former food factory in Geelong to become her export-processing site. She is co-tenant with another food manufacturer making it an affordable option. A private loan has enabled her to fit out the premises. Staff will be employed to run Barton's Smallgoods as a separate entity to her existing farming enterprise at Nulla Vale near Lancefield in Central Victoria. Given the high level of investment to become import ready, she is under no illusion that it will be at least a year before she will enjoy any personal financial benefit.

Preparing for export was an extremely busy time for Toni in 2019, finalising all the paperwork and commissioning the new factory processing plant. She looks surprised when I ask her how she is dealing with the stress. 'I used to be stressed in the corporate world but I'm exactly where I want to be now. I just go into problem-solving mode,' she responds. 'You don't plan to be an entrepreneur. I feel like everything I've done in my life has brought me to this moment.'

In February 2020 I catch up with her as she is preparing to fly to Dubai. 'We've sent off two shipments to Dubai since we last spoke,' Toni says, 'and landed some big accounts in Saudi Arabia, Kuwait, and Qatar.' She explains that 'tasters' have been employed to target some high-end customers and they can't wait to sign up, hence Toni's return trip. 'Apparently I am the face of the brand and they want to see me.'

Two weeks later she returned with orders secured, including with a big five-star hotel chain. 'The sales projections came to $7 million,' says Toni, 'more than justifying a continuation of the export business.' It was full steam ahead until three days later when the international borders started closing and suddenly everything was on hold. Staff were employed on a casual basis until the business got established and did not qualify for JobKeeper. Sadly, she has had to let them go. Toni still has many overheads to pay even while not producing. Despite ticking many boxes for financial support, funding is not as easy to access as the business community is led to believe.

'I'm exhausted,' Toni admits, but she is far from defeated. 'I'm an eternal optimist. I'm using this time to develop new products because it makes sense to have a bigger range on a shelf.' It's also giving her time to firm up her supply chain. 'I realised how vertically integrated I am.' With lamb prices skyrocketing over summer she found that abattoirs were processing fewer sheep and limiting her access to additional lamb bellies needed for her products. Toni has been able to establish a partnership with more farmers, expanding her supply of mutton. Her strategy is simple. 'I pay them a better price.'

www.bartonssmallgoods.com

Keip Filtration

Brendan Earl, Keip Filtration

Twenty-two-year-old Brendan Earl wanted to make his own decisions. It was time to go into business for himself. Fast forward seven years and this savvy young man from Collie in Western Australia is now specialising, expanding his business and has exciting plans for the future.

Like many young men Brendan Earl prefers hands-on learning and didn't particularly like school. Fortunately, being raised in a small business family, he was better prepared for business than others. 'As soon as I could push a wheelbarrow I was working weekends and school holidays for my father's construction business,' he recalls.

After finishing Year 10 he took on an apprenticeship with a local firm, All Tech Plumbing. 'I chose plumbing for the money,' he admits. 'At that time in my life I wanted to do a trade and people said that plumbers get paid the best out of all the trades, I didn't know any better.'

A talent for Australian Rules football saw him playing in Perth for a few years, taking him back to the family business. 'Working with Dad gave me the freedom to travel back and forwards from Perth several times a week,' he explains. A run of injuries put an end to his football career, so he became more focused and, in many ways, this setback helped to launch his business.

'I decided to work for myself, become my own boss,' says Brendan. 'To be honest, at that time I had no real idea about business, so I pretty much winged it at the start and worked hard.' He also found himself an accountant and a bookkeeper. 'We started with a MYOB accounting system, but I now have great admin support and we use Xero which is more efficient and easier.'

Brendan thought that being a local and having a good reputation would give him a head start in his business journey. He was wrong! He quickly discovered that a personal reputation and a business reputation are quite different and he had to work hard to prove the value of his new business. 'It was always hard to get on to tradespeople in a mining boom, so I was on call 24/7 in the beginning trying to break into the market and not wanting to lose a job. It was a bit tough not knowing when your next job is going to be,' he admits.

A lot has changed from his early years of business. Brendan is always open to learning from his mentors and attends numerous business and networking events in a bid to improve and work smarter. 'I understand business a lot better now. I learned by my mistakes and the mistakes of others. It's a great way to learn.'

Brendan noted a growing preference for clean treated water as people become more health conscious, resulting in an increased demand for water filtration. He grabbed the opportunity for a successful business model and Calybre Plumbing & Gas was transformed to Keip Filtration.

'The goal with Keip Filtration is to build an asset and provide a service. For example, on a residential scale anyone can walk into Bunnings or a hardware store and buy a filter then get a plumber or handy man to install it. They don't necessarily know the quality of the product or installer and end up paying top dollar for it; then it's forgotten about,' he explains. 'Keip Filtration provides the full service. We supply only top-quality products at great prices which are then installed and maintained by a trained and licensed plumber.'

By specialising Brendan has transformed his business in a number of positive ways. For a start he has expanded his business base across a wider region, providing water treatment for mines, vineyards and hospitals, wheatbelt farmers and a variety of domestic customers. In fact, the service is now going Australia wide.

By 2018 work had dramatically changed for Brendan. He had a lot more time to work *on* his business rather than *in* his business. 'When you are plumbing you are on call 24/7 but with filtration you can schedule the work, it's not as urgent. This allows me more freedom to build the business, exploring different business ideas and opportunities.' And filtration customers pay better, helping his cash flow. 'A breakdown is not budgeted for,' he explains, 'whereas if a decision is made to get water treated it is planned.'

Scheduling regular filter replacements provides additional customer service. 'When a filter is installed the customer can forget about it. They automatically go on to an automated maintenance program, and I can schedule to suit both the business and the customer.' This adds significant value to Brendan's business. A database has more resale value than goodwill he astutely observes.

In 2018 Brendan won both the Young Business Achiever and Aboriginal Business South West Small Business Awards. He has also benefited from mentoring by Damien Chalk, Director of the Indigenous Procurement Service.

In 2019, with a partner, Brendan explored a new water filtration project on a much grander scale, collaborating to bring new technology to Australia. And after reading an article about high levels of nitrate, uranium and arsenic in water, he started a fund to raise money to treat water for remote Aboriginal communities. As a young Indigenous man Brendan has never tapped into financial assistance. 'I wasn't aware of any financial assistance for Indigenous businesses at the time I started,' he admits, 'but like everything else government funded, it's not just handed to you, you have to jump through lots of hoops. Sometimes it just isn't worth it.'

In fact, Brendan has been lucky enough – albeit through hard work and sacrifice – to self-fund his business right from the beginning, avoiding the need to take out a loan of any kind. With new business plans he hopes to stick with this trend having business savings and a good revenue stream. Having seven years of a successful business makes all the difference.

'Still lots going on with water,' Brendan laughs when we catch up again in 2020. 'Our business trajectory is just growing and growing. Keip has been separated into three distinct business streams: filtration, plumbing and backflow. We're also investing in commercial property and just started a commercial plumbing and waste management company with partners in Perth.' With a growing family Brendan is determined not to become consumed by his businesses. 'I've been reading a lot of books about different business structures and the aim is to have all my businesses self-sustainable and running themselves in five years.'

Reflecting on his achievements Brendan says he is proud to be a young man in business. 'In the beginning it was tough. My friends were making good money while I was just getting by day to day, but I'm in a good position. This is just one step in my journey,' he cautions. 'Collie is where I love to live but the world is a small place. I'm always looking for the new ideas and big opportunities. I like change and I love a challenge.'

BRENDAN'S TOP BUSINESS TIPS:

- Do your research.
- Start.
- Set goals.
- Give it a go.
- Work hard.
- Stick at it.
- Ride the roller coaster.
- Surround yourself with like-minded people.
- Never stop learning.
- Fail fast.

www.keipfiltration.com

Lake Tyrrell Accommodation

Ross Williams, Lake Tyrrell Accommodation

When Ross Williams left his rural hometown of Sea Lake in 1986 for a career, he never envisaged himself returning. Twenty years later he did so, discovering new opportunities for himself and his community.

After leaving Sea Lake in the northern Victoria Mallee district as a young man, Ross worked in research workshops at Melbourne University for almost a decade while pursuing studies through various institutions. With a Social Diploma in Manufacturing & Engineering as well as qualifications in electronics and robotics – 'a mish mash of skills' – he then worked nine years for the TWR Holden Racing Team, taking him to the USA and UK.

Twenty years later Ross returned home to support his ill father. While this was unexpected, the bonus was that his children got the opportunity to know their grandfather before he died three years later. Once back in Sea Lake, Ross looked to generate an income. His first inclination was to stick with his industry and training, but it required too much of an investment. 'Instead I rolled up my sleeves and built two houses,' he explains. 'Then the local electrician couldn't get anyone to work for him, so I did my third apprenticeship. As the business grew, I moved into solar installations.'

Ross noticed a transformation taking place in Sea Lake. Tourists were starting to arrive in their droves to view the acclaimed Lake Tyrrell mirror image at sunset. Julie Pringle who was involved in the region's tourist industry was quick to see the opportunities. She established Sea Lake Tyrrell Tours and started encouraging touring companies to include Sea Lake on their travel itineraries. Rohan Mott, now owner of Sky Mirror Gallery, was also interested in riding this new wave of tourism.

Ross saw an opportunity to fill a gap in the accommodation market and decided to reinvent himself yet again. He is now proprietor of the newly opened Lake Tyrrell Accommodation, providing a contemporary presence at the town's entry. Distinctive domes shelter relocated modern mining units. In addition to providing 20 rooms, there are undercover barbeque and entertainment areas ideal for large groups and bus tours. He also manages three separate villas.

Naturally, getting Ross's new business venture started wasn't without its challenges. 'It's really hard to finance commercial properties,' Ross concedes, but after letting it sit for a while, he was rewarded with a eureka thought. 'I spoke to my mate Rohan, now part owner of the site. Julie, Rohan, his wife Jaqui and I had similar ideas about how we could help grow a secondary economy in Sea Lake; we are all passionate about this project,' explains Ross. 'While it is my design, it is also their inspiration.'

Naturally there were myriad permits and processes to navigate via the local council. With council staff often part time it seemed to take forever. 'While waiting for the paperwork to come through I worked to prepare the site. It all came together just in time for us to open for our first bus booking in March 2019.'

Julie's tour business operates seven days a week from an office and shop in Sea Lake's main street collecting visitors from the accommodation each evening. Rohan stocks a wide range of photographic works in his Lake Tyrrell-inspired gallery. Along with the efforts of a local business network, the trio closely liaise on attracting groups to visit Sea Lake and surrounds. 'We were up in Sydney actively promoting Sea Lake and the region to Chinese tourists and Probus groups,' Ross explains.

By September 2019, the lure of Lake Tyrrell and its magical sunsets, the new silo art trail, and daily trade travel is creating a lot of traffic through Sea Lake. Beds are well occupied at Lake Tyrrell Accommodation as well as the nearby Sea Lake Motel, Royal Hotel and myriad of smaller accommodation houses.

Ross, along with his hometown of Sea Lake, was enjoying the attention before it all changed a few months later. 'We got COVID for a first birthday present!' Traditionally visitor numbers drop when the lake gets dry so the worldwide outbreak had minimal initial impact on Chinese tourists visiting the Mallee. 'We worry about people we have met and hope they are well,' says Ross. 'Bookings did drop off a little more sharply than expected but it's only been a small impact.'

The real impact came a little later, with cancellations from April right through to September 2020, like most others in the hospitality industry. 'We are fortunate not to have a large payroll or excessive debt,' Ross adds. 'We rationalised the way we did things to cater for workers rather than tourists and found some crews to keep us afloat.'

The good news is that the infrastructure works at the Lake have now been completed and, when restrictions allow, there are domestic tourists filtering through. 'The silo art is still a drawcard.'

While the lake generally has water from late May until December, Ross does have a recommendation. 'I like August to November for the classic lake experience. The best colour and salt crystal growth occurs when the ambient temperature begins to rise.'

www.laketyrrellaccommodation.com.au

Agile

Never underestimate the importance of a business being agile and adaptable when it comes to dealing with new competitors, markets, regulations, and a constantly changing environment. As history has shown, no one, not even the well-established and global brands, can afford to be complacent. Need I say any more in a global pandemic?

> 'We had a hunch that this would happen with an awful dry spell last year and two average seasons before that.'

The retirement of key partners can often see the closure of a small business or, with the input of younger family members, it can grow and evolve. With changed government funding imminent due to drought conditions, TMC Enviro in Birchip, Victoria, concentrated on diversifying its business with impressive results that saw them winning major tenders over metropolitan companies.

> 'It's taken me four years to make it and I'm still learning all the time, modifying the show here and there, seeing what works, and the best way to spread the word.'

A passion to live and work in the outback took Tom Curtain to the Northern Territory in 2001. Since then he has experienced an industry collapse, reinvented his business, battled a council, and ignored all his mates who said he couldn't do it. The Katherine Outback Experience started travelling the east and west coasts of Australia and now, in the midst of a pandemic, finds itself having to find new markets all over again.

'We just kept it moving slowly but surely.'

Small businesses can be extremely versatile. They can be scaled up and down according to the times and needs. The Bacchus Marsh Florist & Nursery is currently under the third generation of ownership in the one family and continues to evolve to fit in with family life as well as meet customer needs and restrictions placed on them by a changing environment.

'Selling direct to the public online has been the best decision I've made, for me and my customers.'

With 'Shop Local' campaigns becoming popular, or 'Shop Rural' as I like to promote it, we should also be reminded that many online businesses successfully operate from rural towns. Fair Dinkum Dogs in Central Victoria made the transition from wholesale manufacturing to online retail and hasn't looked back.

'The digital world is not slowing down.'

Underpinning the Think Digital Coach project was Tim Gentle's passion for regional, rural and remote Australia and a clear inequality when it comes to the ability to adopt and use technology. From the moment he won a bus in a competition, Tim has been incredibly agile in developing a business model to fulfil his passion and at the same time help solve a problem for rural and remote educators and industries.

'In the old days the town would roll out the red carpet and offer us the very best spaces at no charge.'

Businesses must evolve and adapt to survive, and no better example comes to mind than the circus. Anton and Simon from Silvers Circus explained to me how it has adopted technology and transgressed from exotic animal acts to highly skilled human acts to meet public demand and take on the challenge of new entertainment mediums. Relax, they still have the clowns!

TMC Enviro

Daniel McLoughlan, TMC Enviro

Small family businesses often end with the retirement of the key partners; or they can continue as younger family members join. Sometimes they can even evolve and grow if prepared to adapt to a new environment, and happily this seems to be the case of TMC Enviro in Birchip. Whether it is drought or pandemic, they are agile and adaptable.

Chatting with TMC Enviro's General Manager Daniel McLoughlan in 2016, the pathway of his family's small business becomes perfectly clear but his parents Tom and Lois probably never anticipated it when they began their shearing and fencing contractor business in the 1980s. Casting his mind back to growing up in the small rural town of Birchip as one of six siblings, Daniel admits he always thought he'd end up in business in some capacity, but it has been an interesting ride.

Without question it began at home when Daniel and his younger brother Tom Junior were encouraged by their parents to be entrepreneurial when as young as eight and 10 years of age. In addition to working for their father in the shearing shed on school holidays, they also developed a substantial lawn-mowing business in town. 'We had quite the lawn-mowing run,' Daniel recalls. 'As it grew Tom went out and bought a ride-on mower and a rotary hoe. Mum and Dad paid our fuel on the provision that we mowed their lawns, but I can assure you it was the last to get mowed, and usually ended up with foot-high grass!'

Each phase of Daniel's subsequent working life in finance, mining and construction, has helped to build the skills he uses today at TMC Enviro. After completing Year 12 at Birchip P–12 School, Daniel took a temporary position at the local branch of the Commonwealth Bank, starting a career in finance. Six months later saw him transferred to Collins Street and ultimately to the head office in Bourke Street, Melbourne. 'I got into personal lending during the property rush, it was a good time to be there,' recalls Daniel.

Three years later, now tired of the office environment, he made the move to Western Australia where he joined two of his brothers in the mining industry. Then it was back to Melbourne where he worked nine years in construction. Each of these jobs was a step closer to his hometown of Birchip, not that Daniel knew it at the time.

Back at home his parents had been transitioning into more of the fencing and rabbit ripping work as Tom senior sought an alternative to the shearing that was taking a physical toll on his body. 'His idea was to work one man on one machine as a sort of semi-retirement,' explains Daniel, 'but he's not a guy who could ever retire. It just sort of ballooned from there.'

In 2011 Daniel was asked to come home to help set up the administration side of the business, which was still being run from the family home. Younger brother Tom had started working hands-on in the business 12 months before. 'I told my girlfriend, now wife, that I would be back in Melbourne in three months but I'm still here five years later,' grins Daniel.

From working with one local Landcare group the business went to two, three, and is now working with up to 16 groups. Catchment management authorities are another big source of environmental work and, of late, the business has been branching out into major project work taking them more widely across Victoria.

It's interesting to reflect on how much has changed over the past decade in the way the business operates. As is usually the case in a country town, it was a simple formula to begin with. 'Dad had a good reputation, the right machinery, and knew a lot of people.'

A good reputation is still a strong selling point, but Daniel points out that it is not always enough when it comes to seeking government contract work, particularly in recent years. 'Just because you are competitively priced and did a good job on the last contract, you don't necessarily get the next one,' he explains. Another important reason TMC Enviro has concentrated on diversifying its business is the fact that government funding is often diverted from budgets, as will be the case with the recent announcement of drought funding. 'We had a hunch that this would happen with an awful dry spell last year and two average seasons before that,' says Daniel.

With this in mind they sought to supplement their local work with bigger projects by employing specialist staff and investing in new work premises, machinery, and an integrated management system. Already it is paying off with a successful tender at the Werribee Open Range Zoo, where they have installed over three kilometres of 4.1-metre-high chain-mesh fencing around the grounds of the zoo's Lower Savannah Precinct. Here a number of the zoo's larger species roam an open-plain environment. Visitors experience this via the Safari Bus Trail, which runs each day. 'Eland look like deer on steroids,' Daniel clarifies before I have a chance to google. 'The fence needs to be extremely high so they don't jump out onto the Geelong freeway.'

I am impressed that a rural family business can compete against metropolitan companies. Daniel tells me that writing a tender submission is a real team effort and reflects their specialist skills. While Tom senior and junior are familiar with the hours and techniques required to complete the work, Daniel is able to contribute his large-scale project-management experience.

Daniel's wife, Melanie Wood, brings several years' HR experience from Melbourne, including the development of policies and procedures, workplace health and safety and HR reporting and statistics, vital to any tender process. Then there is the all-important environmental side of tendering, and indeed their business. On the same principle as a construction company requiring the services of an engineer, TMC Enviro has employed Jess Cook as their Environmental Projects Manager. Jess, who has a Bachelor of Applied Science (Environmental Science), joined the business in 2014.

According to Daniel, the Werribee Zoo project is one great example of how this can be a key factor for success. 'Jess's role was to take environmental considerations into account, including looking at minimising the vegetation clearance, and her environmental background came in very handy.' While constructing a fence seems simple there were other issues to be managed. For instance, the work couldn't be visible when zoo tours were in progress and the crew had to be out of areas by a certain time for animal welfare reasons. TMC Enviro was able to deliver on all fronts. 'Without pumping our tyres too much, it's pretty cool that we are able to pitch ourselves as a one-stop shop,' says Daniel.

Quality assurance is another important selling point according to Daniel, especially as they have a transient workforce for their project work. Tom senior and Tom junior lead a competency training program to ensure that all staff are fully trained and compliant in their systems. 'Our reputation is so important, and Dad literally drives the roads to check up on everything.'

Even with Daniel and Tom junior heavily involved in running the business, it sounded in 2017 as if retirement is still a long way away for Tom senior. But things do continue to change within the business, as I discovered in 2020. Tom junior has now taken on the role of Managing Director of TMC Enviro, with Daniel taking on new challenges outside the business. Tom's partner, Celeste Walsh, who has a Bachelor of Business, heads up the domestic and commercial pest-control arm of the business. 'We're pushing through COVID-19 quite well,' Tom junior tells me in June. 'We got on to safety early. Every employee has a COVID backpack. Separate accommodation and more transport have been provided to keep everyone safe.'

After a conversation with community leaders, TMC Enviro purchased four big hot washing units to sanitise town centres and schools. In May they purchased another Birchip business and operate it under the name of YBS Ag Supplies to keep a valuable service running for the community. 'Apart from a couple of projects delayed by paperwork held up in client offices during the initial shock we've managed to keep all our employees going. We adapted.'

Yes, I guess that is why I already had this business story in this section of the book!

www.tmcenviro.com.au

Katherine Outback Experience

Tom Curtain, Katherine Outback Experience, on the road in Western Australia

A passion to live and work in the outback took Tom Curtain to the Northern Territory in 2001. Since then he has experienced an industry collapse, reinvented his business, battled a council, and ignored all his mates who said he couldn't do it. It was a simple matter of being agile and utilising his talents to create Katherine Outback Experience, which began travelling the east and west coasts of Australia. COVID is yet another story.

Ever since watching *Landline* on the ABC while at primary school in Kingaroy, Queensland, Tom Curtain has dreamed of living and working in the Australian outback. After finishing boarding school, he completed a three-year degree in cattle genetics. 'Mum and Dad wouldn't let me go any sooner,' he admits. But as soon as he finished university he was off to the Territory, living out of a swag and mustering cattle. Yep, he was living the dream!

With a passion and talent for training horses, Tom spent a number of years contract horse breaking throughout the NT and Queensland, travelling from station to station every two to three weeks. Recognising this lifestyle was not sustainable for him and his young family, in 2008 Tom seized the opportunity to purchase a property on the outskirts of Katherine where he set up his own horse-training facility so the cattle stations could send him horses to train. However, in the blink of an eyelid, the 2011 live export ban not only impacted on the cattle stations, it also dried up Tom's business. 'All the budgets were cut on the stations and there were no horses to break-in.'

Fortunately, Tom had one other skill to draw on. 'When I first started mustering in the Territory the head stockman gave me a guitar and showed me how to play three chords.' Ironically this happened while sitting around a campfire, an inspirational place to practise singing and writing songs, as Tom discovered. He subsequently entered a singing contest and won. With no horse training to do, Tom turned to music. 'I started singing at the caravan park four nights a week. Then through conversation people got really interested in what I do and wanted to come and see how I train horses and working dogs. I combined the three and moved into the tourism game.'

Tom had effectively tested and discovered a new business; however, he had to overcome a few obstacles in setting up the Katherine Outback Experience on his property. 'Wearing a cowboy hat gives the impression of being a bit simple. At first there was a lot of negative feedback from my mates,' Tom admits, 'and council said it wouldn't work. I laughed it off and kept on going.'

Apart from talent, Tom had three positive things going for him. 'I knew a little about tourism because my parents operated a farm stay for 25 years, so I had grown up in the industry, offering horse rides to visitors.' The benefits of a university degree also taught him structure, prioritisation of workloads, and to work in a regimental way. And lastly, he knew from experience that audiences like to see something different.

'I won a horse-breaking competition in Queensland a few years ago and, knowing I was also into country music, the commentator asked me to sing. I sang a song while standing on the young horse's back. Thank God I didn't get bucked off!'

The next challenge was to find an audience for Katherine Outback Experience. 'I had to raise awareness that I was here,' says Tom. 'There wasn't much of a budget, so I painted signs on old tin and put them up on the town outskirts. Council said they were too close to the township, so I moved them 70 kilometres out of town.' Tom commandeered the help of mates and backpackers to place brochures on car windshields around shopping centres and caravan parks. 'Facebook came on the scene, which was good, but we had very poor internet, so technology wasn't much use. I had to do a lot of the groundwork face to face.'

Then there was the weather challenge; something that no amount of marketing could overcome. 'Over the wet season, from November to March, Katherine gets too hot and wet to train animals and tourism dries up,' Tom explains.

Using his time productively during the wet Tom initially moved back to his parent's property in Kingaroy where he could still train horses. Then he decided to take his fully trained horses and dogs along too. In 2018 the Katherine Outback Experience is in its second year of being on the road over the summer months, travelling the west and east coasts of Australia, and the business has reached a new level. 'Over the last 15 years I've needed to make extra money to cover my expenses,' Tom explains. 'This is the first year that I haven't had to train horses on the side to make up the difference.'

As you would expect, the logistics are quite complicated when you take six horses and 12 working dogs on the road with a horse truck, caravan, car and trailer to carry all the additional gear such as horse-yard panels and stockfeed needed for four to five months on the road. Locations, permits and publicity need to be negotiated individually with each town he visits.

Thankfully, Tom has some welcome support thanks to a chance encounter three years ago when he met his now fiancé, Annabel, while hitch-hiking in Western Australia. 'Annabel threw in her career as an urban planner in Perth to come and live in a tin shed with me,' Tom says with a look of disbelief and immense relief. 'She's thrown her heart and soul into the business and has taken over the bookings and marketing, which frees me to train the dogs and horses.'

In the first year Tom tested the roadshow concept by booking a two-hectare location for a couple of months in Dunsborough, Western Australia. 'It worked pretty well but we were still missing a lot of tourists and performing six days a week, which is unsustainable.' That's when the show started travelling further afield. 'We thought that by taking the show to regional towns, we could market the event to a resident population four to six weeks in advance rather than having to work tirelessly marketing to the transient tourist market who stay only two to three days,' Annabel explains. 'We also saw an opportunity to partner with local sporting and community groups so they would also profit from the event and help spread the word within their community.'

When I first caught up with Tom and Annabel during a whirlwind visit to Western Australia in 2018, it was evident their business model was working well. St Bridget's Primary School in Collie was doing great business selling food and drinks to a local community out in force for an evening of family entertainment.

The pair works well as a team. Annabel keeps the crowd entertained as Tom prepares to handle a local unbroken horse, explaining his methodology in the process. The dogs are a great hit with the kids and Tom impresses with his horsemanship as he effortlessly canters in a tight circle on a bridle-less horse while playing his guitar and singing. And that's all before he takes to the stage to sing with his west coast sidekick, Big Bob!

'We've done over 30 shows so far this season,' says Tom. 'All at very different venues, everything from cricket ovals to parks and schools. We even did a show at a roadhouse in the middle of nowhere.'

With Annabel administering the website and social media pages, it has become a whole lot easier for people to find Katherine Outback Experience, but Tom is adamant that local relationships are still important in getting the word out to audiences. 'It doesn't matter how good you are, you have to have a good marketing strategy,' says Tom who admits to being terrible at promoting himself. 'It's taken me four years to make it and I'm still learning all the time, modifying the show here and there, seeing what works, and the best way to spread the word.' Whatever they are doing, it has worked well. The Katherine Outback Experience has been awarded the Best Tourist Attraction in the Northern Territory in 2018 and 2019 and took home bronze at the 2018 National Tourism Awards.

Since I first interviewed Tom and Annabel life has been pretty busy for the couple. They have worked tirelessly to build the business while coping with the arrival of Harry.

As usual, during the Northern Territory's wet season, the Katherine Outback Experience was on the road between November 2019 and March 2020. 'We thought we had all our bases covered,' Annabel smiles. 'And then came COVID-19.' While Tom admits to appreciating a break after the road trip, they also had to quickly reassess their business model. 'It wasn't an option to sit back and do nothing,' Annabel says, 'we have livestock to feed and we promised to keep our employees on. In a normal year we would be doing up to 12 shows a week, servicing The Ghan as it stops in Katherine, and putting on shows for business events in Darwin and around the region. Then the borders were shut and suddenly the tourists disappeared,' says Tom.

Instead he focused on what skills he had and put them to work. Tom rang a former boss and immediately received 70 horses that needed breaking, with instructions to 'get cracking'. They also identified a gap in the market with horse-riding lessons in Katherine. 'I work from 4 am until lunchtime breaking the horses then take one-on-one riding lessons from 1 pm until 7 pm.' Tom says that it has been 'a quick win' for cash flow. He is also cherishing the time in the round yards handling the horses. 'I'm developing new methods to try out and assess. And it gives me time to think and write new songs.'

Annabel sees these new activities as an opportunity to grow their team with local employees and accelerate their plans – which include online tutorials featuring Tom's music and horse-breaking skills. They now have 60 first-time riders who are growing in confidence and helping to forge stronger relationships within their community.

Music is still a big part of his life. Following two Golden Guitar Awards in 2018 for his single *Never Never Land*, Tom released a new album and title for the 2019/20 wet season tour, *We're Still Here*. It strongly resonated with his fans. Post COVID-19 the song will have a whole new meaning to a lot of people, and I have no doubt more music will be coming our way.

TOM & ANNABEL'S TOP BUSINESS TIPS:

- Have short- and long-term goals so you know where you want to be and can work out how you are going to get there.
- Be flexible and prepared to take risks. It doesn't matter if it doesn't work; it's a learning curve and will take you one step closer to the next win.
- Surround yourself with positive like-minded people.
- Maintain strong records so you can measure performance and gauge opportunities and constraints.
- Maintain an open mind to allow yourself to keep learning – particularly in a climate where marketing and business trends are changing so rapidly.

www.katherineoutbackexperience.com.au

Bacchus Marsh Florist & Nursery

The changing face of the Bacchus Marsh Nursery, 1975–2000

Small businesses are extremely versatile. They can be scaled up and down according to the times and needs. And there is no better example than the Bacchus Marsh Florist & Nursery currently under the third generation of ownership in the one family.

Josephine Jennings with husband Alf, shortly before she was widowed
and purchased the Bacchus Marsh Nursery

In 1966, only three months after unexpectedly becoming a widow, Josephine
Jennings was convinced by her daughter to have a look at a small plant
nursery advertised for sale in the Victorian town of Bacchus Marsh. Her
husband had worked long-term for the State Rivers Authority, involving
a move from Maffra in Gippsland to Halls Gap in the Grampians. Josie's
duties had revolved around the State Rivers-owned home and raising five
now adult children. Suddenly, left without a home and a husband, it made
perfect sense for her to move closer to where her married daughter Yvonne
Marsden lived in Bacchus Marsh. 'She wasn't very keen on the idea of buying
a business,' says Yvonne, 'but I knew she was gardening mad and the shop
had a residence at the back for her to live in. By the time we had walked
through the shop she had bought it!'

Housed in a small cottage facing the main street, Josie's nursery was
relatively simple. It sold small plants, seeds, fertilisers and pots. The adjacent
shop, also part of the freehold, was rented to a hairdresser. 'Mum did OK
with the business,' recalls Yvonne, who helped out by driving a ute and trailer
to buy new stock from Melbourne when the shop was closed every Monday.

Josie's new husband, Bert Layton, helped out for some time until they got
the travel bug in 1971 and Yvonne and husband Lyle took over the business.
'Lyle thought it would give me something to do now that our three boys were
at school,' Yvonne recalls with a wry smile, or maybe it was a grimace? They

started by leasing, and then purchased the property. For the first six years Lyle worked elsewhere to help pay the nursery off before joining Yvonne in the business full time. Yvonne says the best 11 years of her life were when the family moved into the tiny residence at the back of the shop, so the kids didn't have to go home to an empty house after school.

Within a year the profits had tripled. 'I bought product in much bigger quantities and more lines,' Yvonne explains. 'We also started selling sand, soil and pine bark from the back of the shop and got into horticulture in a bigger way.' Perhaps the biggest change to the business was the introduction of a floristry. 'This ended up providing as much revenue as the nursery,' says Yvonne who taught herself the art of arranging flowers. Land at the rear of the shop was purchased to build their new home and the residence was given over to the business.

The 'big drought' first reared its ugly head in the 1980s and re-emerged in the 1990s effectively shutting down many wholesale nurseries as water restrictions impacted on sales and prompted change. Yvonne and Lyle downscaled the business to its original size and built shops for lease, which has effectively become their superannuation. Lyle was then able to give more time to his passion for farming and training racehorses while Yvonne continued with the floristry and nursery on a smaller scale.

In 2007 their youngest son Brian and his wife Kerryn bought the business. The value of intellectual property and knowledge of customers and processes should never be underestimated. The transition was an easy one given that Kerryn had worked with Yvonne in the business for 15 years. 'It was a great business to go into. We just kept it moving slowly but surely. While some new owners like to promote that their business is under new management, it was carry on as usual for us,' explains Kerryn, who admits to simply telling customers that Yvonne wasn't in today when asked. 'I didn't want to embarrass them if they didn't know.'

Brian is quick to clarify that there were no family favours given in the purchase of the business. 'Mum and Dad have worked hard all their life and deserve a good retirement.' The couple also knew this good solid business had stood the test of time.

But times do change, as do customer expectations and trends. For a start,

Brian and Kerryn introduced seven-day-a-week trading about 11 years ago. 'Rain, hail or shine, we are open,' says Brian. While they employ between four and six staff members at any given time, he and Kerryn work Sundays and public holidays to cut down on penalty rates. 'When we get busy, we get really busy,' adds Kerryn. 'We cater for a lot more weddings these days. People know that we are always open, which is important.'

While the couple have only 'made a few cosmetic changes to the shop' and introduced a few different lines including a lot more indoor plants, there is always plenty to do, especially with regard to the floristry side of the business. 'Flowers are always evolving,' explains Kerryn. 'There are lots of different ideas and trends to keep up with.'

Like most nurseries and garden suppliers, business has been booming with so many people undertaking garden projects during the COVID-19 stay at home restrictions. 'Yes, we've been really busy,' Kerryn confirms when I touch base in mid 2020. 'Lots of home deliveries as per usual and we just had to follow restriction guidelines in the store.'

Their daughters, Jamie and Keely (Josephine's great-granddaughters) also work in the business so there is the potential that one day a fourth generation could be added to this family dynasty of small business owners. Yvonne and Lyle continue to enjoy their retirement despite being a bit cranky when bowls was suspended. 'I am still positive about the future of small business,' Yvonne says.

Whether scaling up or scaling down, or simply doing what it always does best, the Bacchus Marsh Florist & Nursery is a great example of how small business families can live and work where they love over many generations.

THE MARSDEN FAMILY'S TOP BUSINESS TIPS:

- YVONNE: Work it yourself. You have to have staff, but it pays to always be around.
- LYLE: Own your own property.
- BRIAN: Don't spend more than you earn (impressed on him by his mum!).
- KERRYN: Understand that you can't please everyone.

www.bmflorist.com.au

Fair Dinkum Dogs

Elise Brown in her new workplace for Fair Dinkum Dog Coats

With 'shop local' campaigns becoming popular, it is important to be reminded that many online businesses also successfully operate from rural towns. Elise Brown of Fair Dinkum Dog Coats in Central Victoria is just one great example of needing to articulate the story of our businesses so customers can understand who they are supporting. And so they can continue successfully operating during a global pandemic!

Labelled a 'social butterfly' by her parents and teachers, Elise Brown cruised through her school years without accolades. But when her family looks back on her childhood, the signs of an entrepreneur in the making were clearly evident. Always curious, Elise asked lots of questions, and was quick to recognise an opportunity. As a teenager with a strong self-belief she proved herself more than capable of creating her own income. She trained young and difficult horses and sold them to good homes for a healthy profit.

Every day is an opportunity to learn according to Elise and, significantly, her best learning has been outside the education system. While her friends went on to university, she started working in the equine industry, learning on the job and continuing to ask questions of everyone she met along the way.

Elise was supported by her family to purchase a small part-time business, Fair Dinkum Dog Coats, to complement her part-time work. Within six months the 19-year-old was so busy she had to leave her paid job. A year later her family helped her purchase a second business, Midland Stock & Poultry in Castlemaine, as a local retail outlet for her dog coats.

Over a five-year period as a retailer, Elise learnt many valuable skills, including employing staff and balancing stock purchases with cash flow. She also learnt to handle the occasional difficult customer who tried to bully a young person for reasons of their own. As her life circumstances have changed, it has been her first business that has evolved and stood the test of time.

'Fair Dinkum Dog Coats started as a nice part-time business supplying wholesale customers, primarily pet shops, right across Australia,' Elise explains. 'But no matter how hard I worked in advance I couldn't avoid the winter rush and found myself working long hours. It wasn't fun anymore,' she admits, especially when a husband entered the picture and the first of their two children was on the way. Selling the retail store helped alleviate the problem but she still had to find a way to manage the coat manufacture workload.

Elise had a light-bulb moment, demonstrating her problem-solving abilities. 'Despite everyone telling me I was crazy, I wrote to my wholesale customers and told them I was no longer supplying them. I decided to sell direct to customers.'

Cutting off a stable source of income, investing in website development, and learning to manage new technology was a brave move that has fortunately paid off for Elise. By constantly sharing the story of her business and products via social media she has also effectively engaged with customers and avoided costly advertising. 'Selling direct to the public online has been the best decision I've made, for me and my customers,' Elise says. 'Instead of having to produce large orders all at once, I now have a steady flow of individual orders that I can make to each dog's unique measurements, instead of off-the-rack generic sizes.' Recognising the growth in numbers of greyhounds and whippets as pets, she designed a new range to suit their unique shape and this has become a significant proportion of her sales.

Remarkably, despite working fewer hours and selling fewer coats, Elise has tripled her income with the profits coming direct to her instead of being shared with wholesalers. And, most importantly as a young mother, Elise has also been able to dedicate herself to her two small daughters during their preschool years.

In 2019 she was fortunate to receive a $20,000 Digital Champions Grant from the Australian Government enabling her to focus on improving the business. She was also selected by Facebook as one of 30 small businesses to feature in their pre-Christmas campaign. In the lead up to Christmas, posters of Elise appeared in airports and shopping centres Australia-wide to support Facebook's promotional campaign. Her girls thought that was pretty cool!

With both daughters starting school in February 2020 she was excited about the year ahead – until suddenly she found herself home schooling during the COVID-19 shut down. While this slowed her a little, it did not impact the start of the peak selling season, a benefit of being a fully established online store. A new website and a new brand were launched in time for the 2020 autumn season and by all accounts it has been a good year, with sales increasing significantly.

Balancing work with family remains important to Elise, as is maintaining Fair Dinkum's brand and reputation. At the urging of industry advisers, she has explored outsourcing production and exporting options, but keeps coming back to what is important to her: supplying a quality product to her customers. And many customers are happy to share testimonials.

Fair Dinkum Dogs Poster, 2019

Elise believes it is important for the wider community to be educated. 'When people talk about how bad shopping on the internet is, I'd like to remind them that many rural businesses like mine are benefiting from being online,' Elise says. 'Because of the internet I am able to live and work where I love.'

Elise understands the value of explaining who she is and what she stands for. Being nominated for and winning a Victorian Regional Achievement and Community Award in 2010 also gave her a platform to talk about the importance of young people being encouraged to become business owners.

Much to Elise's amazement, she was invited to meet with Queen Elizabeth at Government House in Melbourne during Her Majesty's 2011 visit. A girlfriend provided a quick makeover, but the ever-practical Elise drew the line at changing out of her rubber-soled work boots, which were perfect for walking from Southern Cross Station to Government House.

By sharing Fair Dinkum stories, Elise's customers know exactly who is making their dog coat when they place an order, and chances are it will be posted by two small and very willing helpers who have the privilege of a rural lifestyle thanks to their enterprising mother.

ELISE'S TOP BUSINESS TIPS:

- Create a business that supports your family and lifestyle but understand it's only worth keeping if it is profitable.
- Invest in yourself to keep improving your business.
- Utilise the power of social media to avoid costly advertising.

www.fairdinkumdogs.com.au

DISCLOSURE: As many of you may already know, Elise is my daughter. I'm amazed that it took me so long to write about her!

Think Digital

Tim Gentle, Think Digital

Digital crusader Tim Gentle's passion for regional, rural and remote Australia has prompted his latest challenge to encourage people in digital learning. His new catchcry of 'Get on Board' might be coming to a town near you!

As the finishing touches were being applied in preparation for the official launch of the Think Digital Coach in 2016, Tim Gentle took me for the first on-board tour, explaining why he has embarked on this adventure to take digital education into the regions. It had been interesting to read his posts on social media over the past few months as his latest, and by far most challenging, project took shape. Maybe, just maybe, there were times when even Tim might have felt just a tiny bit overwhelmed?

Tim entered a competition in 2015, putting his case forward with his usual infectious enthusiasm and boundless energy, and duly found himself presented with a coach courtesy of a bus recycle program sponsored by Young's Bus Service in Rockhampton. 'I have my sleeves rolled up, a coach ready for fit-out and a wealth of education to share,' he announced to the world.

A series of photographs record the transformation of the coach courtesy of family, friends and a team of tradespeople, accompanied by a running commentary expressing Tim's overwhelming gratitude and a hint of weariness. Underpinning this project has been Tim's recognition of a clear inequality when it comes to the ability to adopt and use technology. 'Rural people are getting left behind,' says Tim. 'The digital world is not slowing down and I want to help them to keep up. This is why #ThinkDigitalCoach is bringing technology into the region.'

The concept was first sketched 10 years ago in a business-planning workshop. 'None of this happened overnight, a lot of time and energy has gone into it.' His initial concept started with a 4WD vehicle and trailer fitted out with a satellite dish and grew into a full-sized road coach thanks to Young's Bus Service. The coach can be used to host small groups for in-house education as it travels to rural towns and schools. He will also be working with community champions who will have the opportunity to come on board for a week of training.

Tim has over 30 seminar topics that can be delivered in-house or via webinars and on-demand learning. I'm chuffed to learn that as a result of a professional development day that Tim and I collaborated on in 2015 he has developed a new topic – Maximising a Digital Classroom – for teachers and a session for students to engage in a Makerspace session.

So how will it be funded? Tim will work with local governments and corporates who will sponsor the Think Digital Coach to visit their region. Commissions from sales made via the Think Digital Coach program will be placed into a Magic Pudding Fund, the not-for-profit arm of this enterprise. Tim explains that 50% of the fund will be used to provide free internships to Community Champions to enhance their skills and usefulness to their communities, and 50% to maintain and fuel Rocky, the six-wheel coach. Following an initial digital roadshow tour of the Mallee and Sunraysia, Tim took Rocky on the road for several months at a time in various parts of Australia.

When I next caught up with Tim in 2020, Kat Bidstrup had taken on the role of CEO. 'Stepping aside and letting someone else steer the ship took some courage,' he admits, but he is grateful to be able to focus his attention on growing the software side of the business. 'While we still have a passion for regional, rural and remote Australia, we have refined our focus now to develop immersive technologies experiences, using virtual reality and augmented reality, for agriculture. We use this technology to help educate people where their food comes from, inspire people to consider a career in agriculture, and improve efficiencies on the farm.'

To host these resources, a new FarmVR website – www.farmvr.com – has been created. 'We use it to host FarmVR activations at agricultural shows, schools and communities.'

And how is Rocky I wonder? 'Rocky has been amazing,' says Tim. 'Our biggest success story was producing the MLA Lamb Paddock to Plate VR Experience, then taking that on the road across Australia to schools and events, including the major agricultural shows.'

Naturally these activities have been curtailed during coronavirus restrictions, but never one to sit still, Tim has taken the opportunity to develop more materials for the months ahead. 'There is a real thirst from people to understand the technology and start adopting it in their marketing, education and communication. If there is one lesson I have learnt over the past years, it is to listen to my intuition and be on purpose. It takes work and courage, but it is truly remarkable to run a business that is purpose driven. When you are on purpose, amazing things seem to happen.'

www.think.digital

Silvers Circus

Anton Gasser, Silvers Circus

Dating back to the time of the Roman Colosseum, circuses have undergone huge changes – particularly in the last 20 years – to meet public demand and take on the challenge of new entertainment mediums.

When Silvers Circus rolled into my hometown of Castlemaine in 2017, I just had to pop in and have a chat with its owner, the quietly spoken Anton Gasser, and two of his key staff members. Instead of running away to the circus Swiss-born Anton was quite literally born into the circus with a family history of circus performers going right back to the 1600s. With circus blood in his veins and celebrating 40 years since establishing Silvers Circus with his wife Anna here in Australia, there is no doubt that it is as much about lifestyle as it is a business to this hard-working couple and their grown-up children. 'If you want to make money, then don't buy a circus,' says Anton with a wry smile. 'But if you want lots of work and to put a smile on people's faces, then go ahead.'

Anton likens a circus to farming, which is also dependent on weather and the economy. 'We have our good years and we have our bad years. Sometimes we have to go without,' he shrugs philosophically, 'but we make sure our bills are always paid.' The fact remains, where many circuses have come and gone, Silvers is a survivor and I was keen to find out how that has happened.

Simon Tait, Silvers Circus

When I ask long-time employee Simon Tait what the secret is to a successful circus, his answer is clear. 'Location, location, location!' The big top is by far their best advertising; no one can miss it as they drive and walk by. This is a particularly interesting point given that, for the first time in my memory, a circus has been relegated from the town centre to a reserve on the town outskirts with very little drive-by traffic. One of the negative changes he admits, has been the way circuses are received into towns. 'In the old days the town would roll out the red carpet and offer us the very best spaces at no charge; they were just so glad to have us come and provide entertainment.'

But times have changed. Not only are municipal councils now looking to recoup the cost of power and water used, they insist on substantial bonds amounting to thousands of dollars to cover damage that may be incurred to the grounds. Sometimes this is unavoidable due to wet weather and heavy trucks but other times it is a disreputable circus before them that tarnishes the industry image.

Another long-term employee is Margaret Petersen. Melbourne born, she did run away to the circus and has been with Silvers for 35 years. Firmly ensconced in the ticket box, she is in charge of the nerve centre of the circus, efficiently handling the logistics for each town they travel to Australia wide. 'Essentially Margaret has to set up a new business for us in every location,' Simon explains. 'She has to jump through the same hoops again and again.'

'We start with the Victorian Building Authority, then have to get the ground lease sorted, contact neighbours as part of the Good Neighbourhood Code of Practice, and then there is council,' Margaret says, stopping for a breath. 'Not just one department but engineering, OH&S, building and by-laws.'

'Everything goes by the book,' Simon chips in. 'We have to be 100 per cent professional or we go under.' (Well, maybe not the time the monkeys escaped from their enclosure during a sea voyage to Tasmania, which Margaret let slip and I'd dearly love to hear more about, but I digress!)

With all these additional barriers Silvers has had to work extra hard in marketing their shows. Well in advance, like a well-oiled machine, the posters pop up in shop windows and advertisements on television and radio herald their arrival in the region. In addition, there are inflatable clowns on street corners and vehicles with signage strategically placed around town. And then there is the show itself, voted one of the top 10 circuses in the world in 1992.

Silvers gives the external appearance of a traditional circus. The obligatory side-show alley clowns, fairy floss and jumping castle can be found outside. But the program is vastly different. Thankfully Margaret doesn't have to worry about escaping monkeys any more because the circus has transgressed from exotic animal acts to highly skilled human acts. Yes, you will still find the clowns, illusionists, jugglers and acrobats appealing to all ages, but new acts include ones like the Globe of Death featuring motorbike riders who defy gravity and thrill their audiences. I confess I found this very hard to watch, but then again, I didn't like my son riding a peewee at age five either!

Simon believes that circuses are continuing to evolve and there are two main factors contributing to this; the calibre of the international acts and technology. 'The thrill acts are very appealing to the teenage market,' he explains excitedly. 'They come on their own and don't have to be dragged along by Mum and Dad. We are competing with so many forms of entertainment these days that everything we provide has to be a quality act.'

I wonder about safety and how the increasing Occupational, Health & Safety regulations affect circuses? 'We have incredibly dangerous acts, so safety is paramount,' says Simon. 'In many ways circuses have been way ahead of other industries in this respect. These are our family and friends, so we have always worked hard to keep them safe.'

Technology is also a big part of how circuses now function. Far from the old cumbersome canvas tents, the new tent design features only four king poles that can be easily erected and yet withstand gale-force winds. Technology enhances the drama of acts through sophisticated music and lighting.

With lifestyle a major factor drawing people to work in the circus industry Simon reflects on how digital technology has also made life on the road easier for him since starting in his early 20s. 'I remember lining up at a phone box to ring my parents on a Sunday evening to get the cheap STD rates,' he recalls. 'Now I can ring family and friends on my mobile, email or Skype.'

Performing as ringmaster and an illusionist in the show, Simon can also be found helping out with the publicity and driving trucks. 'We all multitask,' he admits. 'You should see me on my day off!'

The more I hear about Silvers Circus, the more it reflects the qualities of any other successful family business. Anton and Anna are clearly loved and respected by their employees, which can number as high as 35 with support staff during peak times. Silvers Circus performers enjoy a month off just before Christmas but another dream of Anton's to provide quality children's entertainment has seen the evolution of a new show especially for the Christmas market. Each year in November and December the big top is now set up at Caulfield Racecourse for Santa's Magical Kingdom.

When I ask Anton to explain the success of his business, he puts it down to teamwork and attention to detail. 'We all work together and, if it's important like making sure your customers have clean toilets, sometimes you have to do it yourself.' While some of the vehicles may be 20 years old, they are meticulously clean, as is the big tent and all the Silvers facilities. This is clearly a source of pride for Anton. 'Silvers Circus is all about quality,' Simon reiterates. 'People are totally entertained and remember the show.'

With a happy audience vacating the big top at the conclusion of its final performance in Castlemaine, the team is anxious to start packing up before setting off in convoy to Ballarat. Performers are shedding their costumes and rolling up their sleeves to lend a hand. From Margaret's perspective, it is all about jumping through all the logistical hoops again, but for Anton it is about seeing the smile on people's faces.

Up until the COVID-19 restrictions in March 2020, it sounded like another exciting year for Silvers Circus. Their website announced that all my favourite Sesame Street characters, including Elmo, Cookie Monster, Abby Cadabby, Bert and Ernie, Super Grover and Big Bird, would be featuring in a brand-new show, the *Sesame Street Circus Spectacular*! In addition to the *Sesame Street* characters, the advertised circus program featured performers from Switzerland, Argentina, Colombia, Morocco, Brazil, Ethiopia and Australia.

'We are all still chilling in ISO at our property in Victoria and we are certainly keeping busy. Lots of maintenance on the big stage, trucks, clearing out old caravans and moving some old trucks,' said a Facebook post in May 2020. Sadly, plans to get my photo taken with Big Bird must be put on hold.

www.silverscircus.com.au

Creative

Every business needs to be resourceful, but we also need to be creative in our visual market savvy world. Carefully crafting our social media posts and marketing materials is a core part of every business, as is telling our authentic stories. Some businesses clearly take creativity that step further, particularly those who work in the arts.

'It had to be chocolate, decadent and made with chickpeas.'

Claire Morgan created Rupanyup Living in response to a long period of drought followed by a severe flood. The community needed a boost and Claire was up for the challenge. Development of the silo art trail across the Wimmera has brought increased business and a new type of customer. Claire came up with the idea for a locally grown product showcasing her local community.

'We need creative care and creative curriculums.'

We often speak about 'getting burnt' in business and it was a memorable occasion when I interviewed Tim Tim the entertainer, who on occasions chooses to work with fire. While my jokes fell decidedly flat, Tim says that the benefits of being a self-employed entertainer are numerous. 'I get to travel, I have adventures, and there is a lot of flexibility and freedom.'

'There are plenty of people doing this type of thing, but I can do it differently.'

Likewise, Shayne Mostyn is looking for the 'wow factor' when tailoring photographic weekend workshops to entice Melbourne customers to his rural hometown of Cohuna. Just before the pandemic restrictions came into force, Shayne launched his new online course. Great timing!

'It enhances our business so we don't charge them to display and sell their goods.'

Debbie Walker combined her love of food and a rustic old engineering shed to create The Old Workshop Café at Anakie, providing a welcome social gathering place for locals and a pleasant stopover for travellers.

'Fabric is my motivation every day. It still excites me sewing two pieces of fabric together to see how they look.'

Thanks to her incredible work captured in a stunning book, *Quilts from the Colonies*, Margaret Mew and her Elphinstone-based business Quilt Station are recognised across the world by quilters.

We can all be inspired by having a creative touch in our business.

Rupanyup Living

Claire Morgan of Rupanyup Living

Why start a small business in a rural town? In 2012, Claire Morgan created Rupanyup Living in response to a long period of drought followed by a severe flood. The community needed a boost and Claire was up for the challenge. But, as she has discovered during the COVID-19 lockdown, the reason you start a business is not always the reason you continue.

Claire and her husband David moved to Rupanyup in 2009. Both from farming families, they were excited to purchase their first cropping property together. 'We wanted to have a go out on our own,' Claire recalls. 'We had a look at this property and fell in love with it. We also wanted to bring our children up in a rural community.'

Right from the beginning they were confronted with challenges. They purchased the property in the midst of a prolonged drought and then watched their rural community endure severe flooding. 'It washed out crops and was financially and emotionally quite devastating for the town.' Add to this a vacant store building in the middle of the main street and Claire's entrepreneurial brain got ticking.

William Cust played an important role in the development of the Wimmera region. He followed the railway line as it was built and opened a general store in each town that sprang up in its wake. In 1872 it was Rupanyup's turn. The original building is long gone, but in the 1980s the local Lion's Club built a replica that sits strategically in the centre strip of the main township. 'It was vacant and looked quite sad,' says Claire. 'It needed a coat of paint, but I could see it was a perfect spot to set up a beautiful boutique gift and homewares store.' With a small rent being paid back to the community, Claire now maintains the Cust's Store building and has developed an outdoor seating area.

An impetus for establishing a boutique store arose from her needs as a young mother living in a rural town. 'With a population of only 500 it is hard to buy nice things, whether it is a gift or something for your home.' With these needs in mind and her experience in retail Claire established Rupanyup Living in Cust's Store. A coffee machine was installed providing a place to gather and chat.

Deciding what products to stock in such a small space has been a balancing act Claire admits. 'As the business has grown it has become easier. At first I saw my role as a support to bring people together and to give back after we were welcomed to the town, but over time I've realised that I'm running a business and I need to make money. I've worked hard and got to know my customers and what rural women like. I've got better at buying the right products for the store.'

Development of the silo art trail across the Wimmera has also brought increased business and a new type of customer. 'Local customers like the candles, soaps, produce, and food hampers. Tourists are more interested in gifts and souvenirs. They want to see something Australian and different, not brands they would see in their shops back at home.'

Claire networks extensively with creatives across the region, attending gift fairs to source products. She also came up with a product idea of her own. 'Our town had been working on ways to promote itself and bring people here. I came up with the idea of a locally grown product that would sit nicely with Rupanyup Living. It had to be chocolate, decadent and made with chickpeas. We are proud of what we grow on our farms and it was an opportunity to share my passion for good quality local product with those visiting.'

Claire played with the recipe for six months. 'Chickpea flour doesn't rise so it works really well with brownies.' She continues to introduce new flavours such as mint, vanilla and chilli and customers can buy their own packet mixes. 'People are so busy. I created a quick and easy recipe for them to whip up at home. The recipe is on the back of the packet. Customers come back for more or buy online.'

Yes, Rupanyup Living is also online! In 2016 Claire realised that the store needed to reach a larger audience to be viable. A marketing business in nearby Warracknabeal helped. 'They did the research, organised professional photographs, and set it up on a Shopify platform. I upload photos of products and it is easy to use.'

Thanks to word-of-mouth referrals and a vibrant Instagram account, destination shoppers come from within a 100-kilometre radius. 'Nothing beats a visit. Have a cuppa, taste the brownies. Enjoy. Then customers can go back to our website.'

Claire makes a point of connecting with tourists as they travel through. 'They enjoy the experience of being in the boutique and I've sensed they want to be closer to our story and our lifestyle. Once that connection is made when they travel through, they can continue buying online and being a part of our community.'

Despite closing their doors during the initial coronavirus lockdown in April and May 2020, online sales remained open. 'We hunkered down and focused on what we could control. I missed a lot of good trade instore for Mother's Day and Easter but there was nothing I could do about it. Home schooling was a priority and we were busy on the farm with cropping. The online store was really busy, which was wonderful. People realised that small rural businesses would be struggling.'

When school resumed and restrictions were eased allowing the store to be reopened, Claire realised something important. 'I was so ready to go back. I realised that I need Rupanyup Living just as much as the community. Living rural, you wear so many hats and the business gives me a break from the farm. This is a role I cherish and love.'

www.rupanyupliving.com.au

Tim Tim

Tim Tim the Entertainer

Businesses know the pressure of customers relying on them but just imagine if you are an entertainer. Not just any entertainer but one that works with fire!

Catching up with Tim Tim over coffee in 2016 he recounted his most recent experience as a self-employed entertainer engaged at the Port Fairy Winter Solstice Festival. Held a week before our chat, the Festival had a fire and water theme and Tim chose fire! 'It was a bit nerve racking,' he admits. 'I just have to dedicate myself to a creative idea and then make it happen. There are weeks of preparation, a long drive to get there, and hundreds of people relying on you to get it right.' Fifteen minutes of fame later and it's all over. Tim is ecstatic; he nailed it. So is the crowd. I'm just relieved. Not a scorched hair to be seen.

A self-confessed 'adrenalin junkie', Tim admits that the more dangerous a stunt is, the more exciting it is. 'If I think of something, I usually make it happen.' Hmmm, I reflect on the word 'usually'. Wouldn't you rather work as a clown I ask? It would be safer, and you could laugh all your way to the bank, I add with a chuckle. One coffee down and I am on fire!

Tim isn't smiling. 'Clowns wear makeup all the time,' he says, clearly wondering where this interview is going. Damn, there goes another potential line: Just clowning around. 'OK' – (audible sigh from me) – 'let's get down to business. How did you get started?' I ask.

It all goes back to an artist in residence at a long-ago Castlemaine State Festival and Tim, at a young impressionable age and struggling at school. 'Greg introduced me to stilt walking and gave me great encouragement,' he says, clearly grateful for this pivotal moment. Tim subsequently took the plunge into a Graduate Diploma in the arts at the Chisholm Institute. He worked for a while in Melbourne making sculptures and imitating art pieces (legally, he assures me), and later travelled the world.

Returning to St Kilda he put his stilt-walking skills back into action for a fundraising performance on the pier. This generated recommendations for gigs for the City of Melbourne and sparked his career path as a self-employed entertainer.

Eight years ago, he was drawn back to his hometown of Castlemaine where his parents still live. 'Economically it makes sense to live in the region,' says Tim who enjoys gardening in his spare time. 'You can have a nice big house with lots of space in comparison to a much smaller space in Melbourne. It's beautiful here. It's clean and fresh, there's good people, and it's relaxed.'

Embracing country life, he has joined the committee of Business Mount Alexander and is enjoying the opportunity to contribute his creative skills as an entertainer and comedian for both adults and children. The benefits of being a self-employed entertainer are numerous, says Tim. 'I get to travel; I have adventures and there is flexibility and freedom.'

On the downside he still has to treat it like a business. It comes as no surprise to me that, as a creative person, Tim has also embraced technology. 'I love technology and I'm always researching on the internet.' With the assistance of friends Tim has set up his own website and maintains it himself, paying attention to optimising google search engines. Invoicing clients with MYOB is a standard task but he does find marketing his business hard work and what he describes as an 'endless well'.

Tim in action at Port Fairy (photo supplied)

Innovative thinking and problem solving are attributes he highly values. He admits his dream job would be to work on Google's creative team! While he waits for this appealing job offer, Tim continues to enjoy teaching himself new skills and making his props for a gig. 'I'm always adding to my repertoire, sometimes redoing old gigs and making them fresh and new.'

Tim is aware of the challenges of working in an outdoor environment and in changing weather, especially when it comes to the spectacular bubble blowing. 'Sometimes the bubbles don't go to plan and other times they are extra magical. It's one of the challenges of the job,' he acknowledges, 'it's gentle and delicate work.'

We touch base again in 2020. While he likes working with corporates and universities, one of his most recent enjoyable experiences was closer to home at Castlemaine South Kindergarten. 'I didn't have to drive, I just walked, and the bubble show was so much fun,' Tim says. 'When I drive to the city, I'm reminded how nice it is to work in the country.'

His latest project is to build a studio to get back into painting and nurture his creative self. Perfect timing with coronavirus restrictions cancelling events he would usually attend. Another of his goals, when it is safe to do so, is to bring creativity into aged-care homes and schools. 'We need creative care and creative curriculums.'

TIM TIM'S TOP BUSINESS TIPS:

- Scope out the market first. Add some research to your gut feeling.
- Enjoy what you are doing. Be enthusiastic!
- Network. Join your local business association.
- Look for the opportunities.
- Have a back-up plan. Don't put all your eggs in the one basket.

Shayne Mostyn Photography

Shayne Mostyn Photography

In what many would term an unusual career pathway, Shayne Mostyn has been preparing to be self-employed for most of his adulthood. From the army to technology, from the Gold Coast to the dairy town of Cohuna, every step and new skill has prepared Shayne to create his own destiny in a town where he was blinded by the stars.

Like most teenagers, school was just something you do every day according to Shayne. 'Nothing inspired me at school,' he admits without apology. 'I just wanted to go into the army.' Six years in the army taught him one of his greatest skills. 'Tolerance,' Shayne says. 'I cope with day-to-day stresses better than most. Like when I'm out at 2 am doing a night photography course with a storm raging around me,' he explains.

Exiting the army, he then became a technician for Xerox in Sydney followed by a stint working at the Olympic Games. 'I worked my way up through Xerox becoming a team leader and then operations manager. You get a name for yourself and then get head hunted to put out fires.'

Working for Xerox and IBM taught Shayne about processes, an important element that has prepared him for business. 'Flying by the seat of your pants is definitely not the way to manage a business,' Shayne says.

Shayne first discovered Cohuna in northern Victoria when he and wife Sarah were visiting her sister over Easter five years ago. Arriving in this small agricultural town they discovered that there was no reception for their mobile phones via Vodaphone. 'Without my usual 140 emails per day, 80% of which would require action, I suddenly had bliss,' Shayne recalls. 'We loved Cohuna and driving back to Melbourne I said to Sarah that I could live there.'

As fate would have it, by the time they arrived back in Melbourne he had received a job offer of driving an excavator. 'I'd driven tanks in the army,' Shayne explains. 'Other than a gun there is not much difference.' Two weeks later Sarah was offered a job with an accounting firm in nearby Echuca, with higher pay than she was receiving on the Gold Coast. Their fate was sealed!

Shayne and Sarah dreamt of owning a farm but it soon became evident that a traditional dairy was beyond their means. 'With a $2.5 million buy-in required we decided to go with a different business model,' Shayne explains. An episode of *Master Chef* featuring goat's cheese gave them the idea to convert an old dairy farm to breed and milk goats, a much more affordable solution.

'I enjoy the farming side of things and did relief milking to gain experience,' says Shayne. 'We're doing something different and I would challenge anyone in the district to say they are bringing in more money per acre.' In light of the 2017 dairy crisis, he is probably right!

With Sarah driving the product development and marketing their boutique soaps made from goat's milk at Windella Farm, Shayne has been free to pursue other interests. It becomes clear he is not one to lounge around at home. That very first weekend in Cohuna he saw the stars and took his first astro shot. Actually, that was a big factor when it came to relocating there. 'You can't see stars like that on the Gold Coast,' he says. 'I started studying online and watching You Tube clips. I took a night photo of an old Massey Ferguson tractor in a paddock and put it up on Facebook where it got a lot of attention.'

That was the catalyst to establishing Shayne Mostyn Photography, now one of his favourite pastimes and an increasing source of revenue as he studies what is the best business model in this field. 'Everyone has a camera these days and, even if they want professional photos, many aren't prepared to pay for it,' he says. As far as photography is concerned, Shayne believes there are three sources of revenue. 1. Selling artwork through a website; 2. Paid photography for special family events and commercial work; and 3. Teaching photography through workshops.

The latter is what Shayne is finding most successful. Collaborating with Matt Krumins, a Melbourne-based photographer, Shayne is offering city photographers something they can't find in Melbourne – the stars. Weekend workshops are bringing city folk to the country. They start with the theory, photograph at night, and then edit and reflect by day.

'We were thinking of doing it closer to Melbourne but because of the dairy crisis and fear in the local community I decided to bring the workshops to Cohuna. It's only eight people each month but it is eight people who weren't visiting before,' Shayne says. 'They come and stay in the local accommodation and spend their money in town.'

Becoming part of a rural community has had a huge impact on Shayne and Sarah. 'On the Gold Coast we lived close to people but didn't know anyone. Here we have got to know people. What should take 30 minutes to do often takes over an hour in Cohuna because we are always stopping to talk.'

And local connections lead to more work, as Shayne has discovered.

Drawing on his technical skills and love of a challenge, he has his finger in many pies. Twenty-five local businesses now entrust their websites to Shayne for regular updates and he is also trained as a specialist hoof trimmer for local dairy farmers, requiring training in the United States.

Clearly Shayne relishes living in a rural town.

'There is an element of satisfaction and achievement I've never had before,' he admits. 'I'm more creative. I look at an opportunity and see what I can do with it.' On the downside there is limited customer reach in a rural town. 'You're also competing with the locals who are already well known.' Once again on a positive note, he adds, 'The strength of a small town is word-of-mouth testimonials. Do a good job and they become your biggest advocate.'

Five years living in Cohuna and Shayne's goal is not to be working for anyone else. That means doing something different, hence the astroworkshops and a new idea to combine them with a tour of the Murray River. 'There are plenty of people doing this type of thing, but I can do it differently. I'm looking for the wow factor,' Shayne says.

Did Shayne have stars in his eyes when he set these goals? I catch up with him in 2020 to find out. While the astro workshops continue to be run when rain and cloud permit, Shayne admits that his iPhone workshops are proving to be the most popular. Why I wonder? 'Everyone has an iPhone,' he replies. 'The main groups of people that come are young mothers, grey nomads and business owners. It's all good fun.'

Shayne has also found web design – both new work and ongoing maintenance – with local businesses to be good regular work. 'My customers are mostly local businesses. People like the fact that there is a face and someone to answer the phone.' With wife Sarah also busy with Windella Farm, her goat dairy business, Shayne has been helping out with new marketing initiatives on social media. He starts to tell me his latest news then suddenly pauses. 'I'm branching out on a different tangent and busy building something new, but its hush hush,' is all he will say.

My curiosity is heightened, and he relents. 'It's an online version of my iPhone photography workshops,' he confides. 'They have been very popular locally, so I am taking it online to a wider audience.' What excellent timing with coronavirus restrictions coming in a few weeks after this conversation. Has it been a good move to Cohuna? I ask again. This time he doesn't hesitate. 'We love it here.'

SHAYNE'S TOP BUSINESS TIPS

- Diversify. Don't do what everyone else does.
- Follow up with everything you do.
- Be honest about what you can do.

  www.shaynemostynphotography.com.au

The Old Workshop Café

Debbie and Krystal Walker, The Old Workshop Café

There is something about a corrugated-iron shed that attracts the eye. Iconic markers on our rural landscape, they serve so many purposes, from shearing to hay storage and mechanical works. Regardless of searing heat and bitter cold they are places of shelter and productivity. But what takes place within those spaces is changing as indicated by The Old Workshop Café at Anakie between Geelong and Ballan. When my eyes were drawn to an old shed with a vibrant new look about it, I couldn't help but stop off to find out more.

Good coffee and a place for social gathering are essential ingredients of any rural town and Anakie (population 690) is no exception. Local businesswoman Debbie Walker has put her accounting skills, chef daughter, and an old engineering shed to good use creating a quality café featuring organic produce for locals and travellers along the Geelong Ballan Road.

That's the short version. It has been a much longer journey and, like every small business, fraught with challenges. But Debbie is justifiably proud of her achievement and the opportunities it has brought her small community. For 25 years Debbie and husband Bob operated their engineering works on this site. As more equipment was acquired and they reached full capacity for electricity, it was time for a move. Adjacent land was purchased, new larger premises were purpose built for the engineering works and, suddenly, the old workshop was vacant.

Two years earlier Debbie had established a small café on the opposite side of the road. 'I've always been passionate about producing my own food and cooking,' explains Debbie. 'When Krystal, our chef daughter and mother of four, started looking for some part-time work it was perfect timing.' The vacant old workshop promised more floor space, off-road parking and an opportunity to showcase organic vegetable beds and fruit trees as part of the café landscaping. With their café experience, Debbie's planning skills, and Bob's engineering expertise to fit it out, it should have been a simple transition. Like many small business owners caught in that time warp of investing large amounts of money and keen to get trading as soon as possible, Debbie discovered otherwise.

'Dealing with council without a doubt,' Debbie says when asked what their biggest challenge has been. 'We expected help because we were encouraging employment and attracting tourists,' says Debbie, 'but couldn't get a straight answer when setting up the disabled toilet. It took 12 weeks to find out where a handrail should go.' She soon discovered that it was quicker to get information from other sources. 'After two years of fighting and having spent too much time, effort and money, I just couldn't back down.'

Debbie found the Health Department much easier to deal with. Proudly she shows me behind the scenes in their spotless kitchen and cool room.

'The department has stringent health and safety guidelines which we gladly adhere to. We have one of the cleanest commercial kitchens, a fully trained chef, and all of our staff undertake a food-handling course. When things go quiet with customers everyone knows without being asked to scrub under the benches and check behind the doors.'

Until coronavirus, 10 casual staff were employed by the café, which opened Friday to Sunday. 'They come from near and far,' Debbie says. She translates that to 'some staff live just up the road while others travel up to 15 kilometres'. Working in hospitality is not for everyone she cautions. 'I have to be careful to maintain relationships in a small town and encourage potential employees to come and talk first.' For those who do have people skills it is a great training opportunity.

It goes without saying that customer service is paramount in hospitality and Debbie is constantly thinking of ways to make customers feel more comfortable in an open shed. 'We get the fire going when it's cold, and on hot days use lots of ice, cool the glasses in the fridge, and bring out the big fans. People realise that we're trying to make them as comfortable as possible.'

She admits it's a tough industry. 'It can go from no customers to 10 cars pulling up simultaneously. One day it was so hot, and we were absolutely dead business wise, but still had to have full staff. We cleaned out the storeroom, tried out some new recipes and made a big batch of beetroot relish. We got so much done!'

Being part of a small community brings many benefits. While the café provides an important space for locals to gather and socialise, it also provides an outlet for local producers of flowers, honey, olive oil, and even handmade glass necklaces. 'It enhances our business, so we don't charge them anything to display and sell their goods. My only stipulation is that they have to make it themselves,' explains Debbie.

With an accounting background and 30 years of experience in the family engineering business, Debbie has no illusions when it comes to investment. 'You have to spend money to make money,' she advises, 'and you can't expect to retrieve your investment in the first year.' As is often the case, the best of budgets and time schedules can blow out, but the Walkers keep forging ahead regardless. In one extreme example, a sewerage plant was budgeted at $5000 but cost $28,000. 'It means that our decking has to wait a bit longer,' she shrugs philosophically.

As The Old Workshop Café entered its second year of trading in 2018, Debbie was feeling satisfied with their achievements. Their customer base had grown requiring an overflow car park. 'Not a bad problem to have,' she smiles. Likewise, the garden has grown significantly. 'It's a great pleasure to give the menu a twist on a regular basis to incorporate the seasonal produce from the garden.'

The car park is almost full when I pull into The Old Workshop Café in January 2020. Debbie is busy serving and chatting with customers. Krystal and the staff are busy behind the counter. New local wares are on display and it looks as if much has been added, including vintage motorcycles. Bob walks over while I'm admiring a rusted army truck cab adjacent to the café. He explains his latest project. 'I'm just fixing it up a bit so the kids can sit in it and pretend they're driving.' Likewise, a boat and mock train are ready to be clambered over. 'It gives them something to do.'

What I am most interested in is a beautiful old timber bench that can easily sit 10 people. 'I bought it from a neighbour's clearing sale. He got it from the Victorian Railways where he used to work,' Bob says, showing the pock rivet marks still visible in the bench top. No chance of anyone stealing this as it took a forklift to put it in place!

'We always have plans for more to be done but the staff, service and food are exactly where I'm happy,' says Debbie. 'We're not big business, we are part of the community.'

DEBBIE'S TOP BUSINESS TIPS:
- Don't borrow.
- Be brave. Don't be scared to make a decision.
- Enjoy what you do. If you love it, it's not work.
- Be a part of your community.

www.facebook.com/dashfoodstore

Quilt Station

Margaret Mew, Quilt Station

Margaret Mew can't remember a time when she hasn't made 'fine little things'. As a teenager she made her own clothes, then she sewed and knitted for her children ... as mothers often did. Then, in 1992, she went to a patchwork class and her world dramatically changed. Today, thanks to her incredible work captured in her stunning book, Quilts from the Colonies, Margaret and her Elphinstone-based business Quilt Station have an international reputation among quilters.

Why patchwork I ask? Margaret barely pauses to answer. 'I loved that it had unlimited possibilities of pattern, of colour and prints of fabric,' she explains. And over 20 years later it appears that she is still mesmerised. 'Fabric is my motivation every day. It still excites me sewing two pieces of fabric together to see how they look.'

Like all artisans Margaret has dedicated years to learning her craft and the journey has been an interesting one. Her newfound passion, fuelled by continued attendance at patchwork classes, led to her, and others, founding Goldfields Quilters and she started working part-time at a patchwork shop in a nearby town. 'Some days I just got paid in fabric,' she admits with a wry smile. She then started taking in-house classes at the shop, conveniently attracting more customers to buy fabric.

After a 10-year 'apprenticeship' in quilting Margaret started producing her own patterns, with an emphasis on the traditional antique American styles she particularly loves, and selling them in-house and through the shop's website. It can be quite a long process. Margaret begins by making the quilt, then calculates the technical instructions and produces it as a physical pattern for quilters to purchase. 'In the early days I literally drew the diagrams with handwritten instructions and photocopied them,' she explains. 'The early ones looked pretty basic but slowly and surely I've gained more computer skills and now I'm using a graphic designer and producing them with a bit more of an edge.' Her most recent pattern was printed in full colour and retails for $32.

According to Margaret matters became really exciting around 2010 when a quilting shop in the Netherlands started buying her patterns wholesale and Margaret's name started appearing in European quilting circles. In 2011, staff from France-based magazine and book publisher Quiltmania visited Australia for a Sydney event. Carol the publisher and Guy their photographer travelled to Elphinstone, artfully 'threw' quilts around Margaret's house, and took beautiful photographs. Over the next few years *Quiltmania* magazine featured Margaret in articles and published some of her patterns.

It was time for Margaret to capitalise on this worldwide recognition, only enjoyed by a handful of Australian quilters. She left her part-time job and purchased a long-arm quilt machine business that she could operate from home. Not only did this unique piece of machinery assist her to finish her own quilts, it enabled her to take on work from hobby quilters in the region, providing a small but steady income. Her first task was to write to the previous owner's customers introducing herself. Quilt Station in the tiny Central Victorian township of Elphinstone was born!

The year 2017 was another significant milestone when Quiltmania published *Quilts from the Colonies* by Margaret Mew, with text in both English and French. Margaret enjoyed an all-expenses-paid trip to France to attend the launch. 'I sat and signed books for four days followed by a lovely holiday,' she smiles. She also travelled to the United States, promoting the book and teaching even more obsessed quilters in what is reputedly a US$3.7 billion annual industry, according to figures published by the International Quilt Market.

Despite this incredible international publicity, it remains up to Margaret to generate local marketing and publicity to keep a steady flow of income. She maintains her own website with a creative eye. 'I am very particular about how everything looks and am constantly changing my website,' she admits. She is also an avid blogger and has recently embraced Instagram and is already enjoying a huge following. An online course has encouraged her to update her profile and better connect with potential customers. 'I don't think I could have built my business without social media,' she admits. 'All quilters are on Instagram, which is so good for creatives because they are so visual.'

With experience Margaret is becoming more strategic in converting followers to customers. 'You need to let people in, connect with them and build a relationship by offering something for free,' Margaret explains. 'Once I have guided them to my blog where I talk in more detail, they are then on my website with access to my shopping page.'

While the long-arm quilting machine was a major factor in her initial business, she now concentrates on her more favoured activities, speaking and teaching, both of which help promote sales of her book, patterns and templates. A glance at her online calendar reveals that she is a regular guest speaker at guild events across Victoria and interstate, in addition to her own fortnightly in-house classes. Margaret clearly enjoys this and it helps fund another of her passions, overseas travel! In October 2018 she was off on another quilting adventure spanning the Netherlands, France and the United Kingdom.

What surprises me most is that Margaret rarely sells a quilt, instead keeping them for teaching purposes. Quilts are only sold when her cupboards get too full and then sales are usually to friends and for only a fraction of the cost that it takes to produce them. As an accredited appraiser who volunteers at guild events to enable quilt owners to apply for insurance cover, she clearly understands their value. 'It's not unusual for a handmade quilt to be valued at $5000 or even $8000,' she says, 'but that doesn't mean that someone will pay that.'

Margaret also has a large collection of old fabrics that are exceeding storage space and is looking at selling them through a booth in the United Kingdom. This strategic decision will help her gain new customers for her patterns and teaching classes.

One of the biggest challenges of being a home-based business, especially one that grew from a hobby, is that her friends don't understand she has work to do. 'Every day is a workday when you work for yourself,' acknowledges Margaret, who is busy producing new works for patterns and hopefully a second book.

Margaret follows guild and council standards when she speaks and charges fees she is comfortable with. She also maintains the books for her husband's business, Art Station, based in the outbuildings at their home. Although the two businesses are kept separate in an online accounting system, Margaret is grateful that they come under the one partnership requiring only one BAS to be completed for taxation purposes. She is under no illusion. 'Quilt Station is not our main source of income,' Margaret admits, 'but the bottom line is that I will always make quilts because it's what I love to do. It also gives me amazing opportunities.'

An email pops into my inbox late at night in February 2020. 'I'm currently in Sussex in a 400-year-old cottage about to light the fire for the day in an inglenook fireplace,' Margaret writes. 'Earlier I cooked scrambled eggs on the old AGA range. I'm gazing out the window at the open fields.' Now I am jealous!

'Yes, huge changes to the business,' she responds to my question. 'I travel for tutoring a lot now, averaging two trips to Europe and UK per year, each trip about a month. This current trip alone sees workshops in Kent in the UK, France, Belgium and Netherlands.' Each year she takes up a booth at the Festival of Quilts in Birmingham to sell her patterns, fabrics and templates for her unique quilt designs. But plans to return to the United Kingdom in August for more tutoring and on to the USA for tutoring and appearances have been put on hold thanks to coronavirus.

In exciting news, she is working on a second book for Quiltmania France to be released at the end of this year. 'My machine quilting business has been wound up and I focus on tutoring internationally and interstate, quilt design and the additions of patterns, fabrics and templates to assist customers to make my quilt designs.'

A threefold increase in her Instagram following since we last spoke is impressive. 'This continues to be my main source of connecting with my customer base, especially internationally,' Margaret explains.

Sounds like all that hard work has paid off and, thanks to the internet, Margaret continues to have a global audience to tap into, even if she has to stay put in Australia during the remainder of 2020.

www.quiltstation.com.au

Collaborative

Rural people understand why it is important to support each other. No business is an island. If another business is successful, it increases the chance of your business's success. We are each other's customers; we help to attract new customers to our local community; and we support each other when a helping hand is needed.

Collaboration can take many forms, such as partners forming a business, multiple businesses working together on a big project, the co-location of businesses in the one space, or the popular cooperative model often used in rural towns. It can also be as simple as the sharing of freight or promotional costs and mentoring.

Clearly there are challenges, especially when it comes to the different personalities and skills sets within a collaboration. There is a need for plans and roles to be documented and, when necessary, legal agreements to be drawn up to protect all parties. I hasten to add that this includes family members. It is also important to have an exit plan for partners and members if their circumstances change or things don't work out. But often they do and hopefully these stories will inspire you to consider your own form of collaboration.

'You need to recognise the points at which you are competitors and where you are not.'

When pork producers in the Cohuna district were faced with an increase in freight costs for purchasing feed, Aeger Kingma, an enterprising pig grower with a passion for 'crunching numbers', decided it was time to take action. Five growers subsequently established Pentagon Feeds Pty Ltd, which significantly reduced costs for its partners and within six years was earning them a healthy profit.

'We all have our strengths. Some are working behind the scenes but we're all putting in.'

A group of farmers, teachers, truck drivers and community leaders in Wycheproof knew nothing about running a bakery but decided to do it anyway because that is what their community needed. Despite the many challenges and a steep learning curve, they have proven that a group of people with a diverse range of skills and a vision to strengthen their community can make a start-up business not only achievable but a success.

'Young and old worked together for seven months. Counting our volunteer contributions, we have invested $5 million so far.'

When Sea Lake's hotel burnt down and the only other pub in town was closed, action was clearly needed. Local resident, John 'Bull' Clohesy, picked up the phone and started calling. Forty-two investors in the Royal Hotel Cooperative purchased the dilapidated property at auction and gave it a new future.

'There was no way I could afford to open a store all by myself. I started thinking that perhaps there were others in similar circumstances.'

As home-based businesses gather traction with their online retailing, another need emerges when customers seek access to a physical storefront. Solving a problem for one such rural online business has resulted in a great outcome for the small town of Quambatook in the southern Mallee of Victoria. Welcome to the Quambatook Share Shop!

'Bailey isn't a morning person. I do the morning chores and most of the infrastructure stuff.'

We've all heard the saying that it takes a village to raise a child, however the Cohuna–Leitchville district in northern Victoria has taken it a step further. They are nurturing and encouraging young entrepreneurs! I loved interviewing students Cooper and Bailey Taylor about their business, 15 Acres.

'Adam was already a big name in the industry in the United States so it was good to have his endorsement and for him to be part of the business.'

Embracing the digital world, 18-year-old Brendan Murphy collaborated with a fellow fitness fanatic in the United States to create AMPLIFTS, an online fitness program.

Pentagon Feeds

Aeger Kingma, Pentagon Feeds (Courtesy Shayne Mostyn Photography)

When a small group of pork producers was faced with an increase in freight costs for the cost of purchasing feed, enterprising pig grower Aeger Kingma was motivated to take action. Five growers subsequently established Pentagon Feeds at Cohuna, in northern Victoria, in 2010. Six years on and it has significantly reduced costs for its members and is turning over $20 million per annum.

Comprising a green site development of a purpose-built feed processing mill with capacity to store 3000 tonnes of grain, Pentagon Feeds is a substantial addition to Cohuna's industrial district. The mill produces 1000 tonnes of pig feed a week to meet the needs of its five shareholders and other local pork producers. By controlling their own grain procurement and utilising modern technology to achieve efficiencies, this privately owned company is producing quality feed at a reduced cost.

Aeger is happy to share why he believes Pentagon has been a success. In his view, it all comes down to 'a bit of lateral thinking and an ability to crunch the numbers'. As is often the case in agriculture, he also agrees that adversity is a good catalyst for change, enabled through a spirit of co-operation. 'For a couple of years, the pig industry wasn't so good and there wasn't a lot of money in it,' explains Aeger. Given his long involvement in the industry as a current director of Australian Pork and former representative of the Victorian Farmers Federation Pig Group, he is well placed to comment.

'Changes to the pork industry import regulations in the early 2000s allowed importation of pork into Australia which ultimately decreased pork prices and resulted in an excess of pigs being produced. A number of pork producers exited the market until the national herd was decreased and a balanced industry and pricing was restored in economic terms.' Then, just as balance was being restored, along came the drought. 'This increased our feed costs and impacted severely on our bottom line,' says Aeger.

Normally 50–60% of total costs, feed costs rose as high as 75% in the drought. When their local feed mill closed down in 2007 an additional freight impost was introduced to transport feed from St Arnaud. As a producer who runs 1400 sows and cares for a total of 14,000 pigs at any time, Aeger had good reason to be concerned. 'We had no control and were fed up with being dictated to.'

Using his accounting skills, Aeger wrestled with the issue and came up with a business proposal based on a similar model in South Australia. Operating for about a decade, the Murray Bridge Abattoir, led by Ian Parish, had successfully brought together a group of farmers and processors to control the quality of slaughtering for the export and domestic markets. 'It was initially Ian's suggestion that we look at this model,' says Aeger. 'A proposal was prepared but none of us had a lot of spare cash at the time, so we parked the idea for a couple of years.'

In 2009 the timing was right. Aeger updated the figures and put the proposal to five local pork growers. Most of the group already had a relationship for joint negotiations to purchase feed at the best price. In fact, with this existing spirit of co-operation, Pentagon Feeds Pty Ltd only took 17 months from the initial concept to turning out the first run of feed pellets. 'We worked out that we could build a pretty fancy mill for the cost of freight savings and produce at least 600 tonnes of feed per week for ourselves and other customers.'

Initially each partner signed an Expression of Interest and contributed $2000 to fund a feasibility study to ensure the proposal was sound. Discussion then turned to operating budgets and the legal side of the business, with agreements drawn up on how profits would be distributed and shares could be traded or sold.

Because the amount of feed required for each partner varied, shares issued was proportional to the amount of feed consumed. This was an important part of the company structure so it was considered fair that the shared risk be proportional according to the shareholding. 'We each put in cash to underwrite a loan for the business. All up we borrowed $3.2 million. The bank co-operated with us to establish proportional guarantees.'

Aeger stresses the importance of having a champion who will drive the process. 'You need to recognise when you are competitors and when you are not. It's then easy to create a desire to achieve as long as someone is prepared to lead it.' Aeger took the time to make a personal approach to each grower, explaining the figures and assisting them to understand the required investment versus anticipated return.

Early on the shareholders decided on a few basic principles. 'We agreed that we were sharing the mill and that we would be as efficient as we could be, which meant compromise. Efficiency depends on long production runs with similar rations, not lots of different varieties.'

Six years down the track and Aeger, who was appointed non-voting part-time executive director, is clearly delighted with the results. 'It's gone significantly better than expected. We bought into the concept based on savings on freight but didn't understand the savings generated by being involved in our own procurement of raw materials, which were obtained at a cheaper price than by the previous supplier.'

The mill was designed to be run with low labour input and, with the unanticipated savings on procurement, Pentagon has been able to weather the storm of increased energy costs. Aeger proudly claims that they get 33% throughput above the average of other mills out of their presses and can recite a range of statistics and figures to back it up.

Strategy is an important part of each board meeting held every two months, especially when it comes to purchasing their main raw ingredient of grain. 'If commodity prices are at a high point, we buy short, and if they are at a low point we buy long,' says Aeger. 'We are lucky to have the funds behind us to buy six months' worth of grain.'

The company has just invested in additional grain storage to maximise buying capacity. They now have eight silos with capacity to store a total of 3000 tonnes of grain for processing. As a director of Pork Australia, Aeger also follows with interest the results of any research. Specialised equipment from Germany enables Pentagon to precisely measure and add protein to food pellets, once again maximising available raw materials for the cheapest possible ration cost. 'Fat is a good source of digestible energy,' explains Aeger. 'Every percentage point of energy is worth about $28 per tonne to us.'

An infrared machine, the size of a small computer, gives Pentagon the ability to scan incoming samples of grain and translate the imagery into data that is then emailed to their nutritionist for analysis. It cost $70,000. Another device accurately sprays additional fat coating around the food pellets. A nutritionist uses the information derived to formulate appropriate rations for each class of pig.

Six years on, and with all this additional investment, there is no doubt the benefits have been significant for Pentagon Feeds' shareholders. 'More than $1 million per year finds its way back to shareholders or into assets,' says Aeger. His accounting background compels him to measure and track his own savings. 'I personally save $5000 each week on supplying feed to our farm.' He is aware that the longer they are removed from purchasing through a feed supplier, the more difficult it will be to calculate an accurate return. 'It's not just the freight savings, it is the increased ability to control the quality of feed going to your animals.' Their next challenge as directors is to manage a new, and most welcome, scenario as the company transitions from one that has a big debt to service to one that doesn't.

Without doubt, Pentagon Feeds is a great success story. As long as there is a viable pork industry, Aeger does not foresee any changes in his lifetime to the company structure or its shareholders, despite an exit strategy being clearly outlined from the start. 'All five shareholders are well into succession planning,' says Aeger. 'My son is well entrenched in our piggery business and while it exists the need for the mill exists.' If there is a downturn, the mill infrastructure can be adapted to process feed for another species.

He is still sounding pleased when I touch base with him in early 2020. 'The model we developed has all transpired,' he tells me. 'Shareholders have a great investment which is continuing to prosper for them.' While all the original shareholders continue to be involved, one is now in the process of retiring and selling his shares to a nephew who is already a shareholder. 'The structure is managing our succession well,' Aeger concludes.

A double in the capacity for grain storage onsite has also been a good investment as grain prices are set to increase. 'It's been a hard year in some respects,' says Aeger, 'but there have still been some good crops about.' We get on to general chit chat and the number-crunching pork producer lets slip that he's also in the process of retiring from his pork growing business and looking forward to some travel with wife, Ann. Ouch. Could have been better timing in a pandemic restricted year!

AEGER'S TOP BUSINESS TIPS:

- Understand where control can bring added profit to your business.
- Think strategy before structure.
- Commit the necessary number of people to make it viable.
- Recognise the points at which you are competitors and where you are not.
- Take the personal approach when convincing others about a business idea. Explain the vision backed up by the figures and how they work.
- The simpler you can keep it, the easier it is to get off the ground.
- Be clear on your exit strategy before agreeing to entry.

Bakery on Broadway

Bakery on Broadway partners

What do farmers, teachers, truck drivers and community leaders have in common? They're partners in the newly opened Bakery on Broadway in Wycheproof of course!

Wycheproof on the Calder Highway is a close-knit agricultural community with a population of 789 and a strong volunteer component that works hard to support itself. Social events to bring the community together are immensely popular and it was on the day of the 2013 Wycheproof Cup that Amanda Gretgrix mentioned the appeal of having a local bakery. Schoolteacher Chris Duffy, to whom her comment was directed, readily agreed, as did others. In fact, the conversation progressed so quickly that four local couples committed to the finance and purchased a building within a month, just before Christmas!

Chatting with some of the partners more than two years after this momentous decision, it becomes clear that purchasing the building was the easy part. One of the advantages of rural real estate is that it is far cheaper to purchase than in the city. Despite their best intentions, however, the bakery didn't open its doors until Easter 2016. 'So many people kept asking us why there was a delay,' says Ann. 'It was very frustrating for us all.'

Bakery on Broadway is now open and thriving, and I wonder what they have learnt along the way. Working on a set budget, the partners undertook as much of the work as possible on weekends and in and around their daily work commitments. While structurally sound, the 1897 heritage building needed considerable refurbishment to become a modern bakery. 'We cleaned 100 years of dust out of the roof cavity,' recalls Marcus.

An architect worked with them and local contractors were hired to complete the electrical, plumbing and concreting tasks that were outside their skill set. But it was regulations that apply to a building changing business purpose that held the project up the most. 'While we had always planned for all-abilities access, we hadn't anticipated some of the extra requirements, so it took a bit longer to sort that out,' explains Ann. Amanda points out how wonderful the access is for their customers. 'On our very first day we had a young boy in a wheelchair come into the bakery without assistance. You don't realise how difficult it is for many people with mobility issues in rural towns right along the Calder Highway.'

When it came to sourcing equipment a relationship between a local club and Wycheproof Township provided an unexpected helping hand. 'David Bourke from the Keilor Rotary Club was wonderful,' says Ann. 'When he heard what we were doing, he found a company in Melbourne that was able to mentor us through the process of setting up a bakery and purchasing the right equipment at the right price.'

Recruiting skilled staff required lots of networking to find the right people. The outcome has been positive with a qualified baker relocating from Melbourne to Wycheproof. His family and a nephew are about to follow. In addition, a trainee pastry chef and barista have been employed through the visa scheme, also moving to rural Victoria in the process.

And it has been good news for the locals. Not only do they have an exciting new venue for coffee and food, the bakery has created 13 jobs with potential for more as the business starts to provide a return on investment and the partners step back.

When 25-year-old Cobie presented for an interview she had no idea she was going to be offered the position of manager. 'No staff should have to answer to eight different bosses, so we decided it was best to appoint a manager for the Monday to Friday shift,' says Amanda. 'If Cobie tells me to wash the dishes then that is what I do.'

This enterprise has been a real team effort by the partners, each placing their own stamp on the building, always practical and sometimes creative. Ann thought that the history was important so wrote a blackboard history for visitors to read. Nikkie and Adrien created the stunning outdoor furniture utilising old pallets and truck axles. 'We all have our strengths. Some are working behind the scenes but we're all contributing,' explains Ann. Amanda agrees. 'The men took on the majority of the work in the building phase but now the bakery is open it is my time to help out.'

In these early stages, the partners are hands on in the business working the weekend and early morning shifts as well as taking on tasks. Adrian opens at 5 am each morning for the bakers and Marcus cleans each night after closing. Darren the truck owner–driver takes care of freight. Nikkie makes slices and Chris (aka Duffy) does the daily float. Ann liaises with the accountant while Amanda looks after social media promotion. Christine, Principal of Wycheproof P-12 College by day, picks up any number of small tasks out of school hours.

As in any small business, extended family members have been recruited to assist wherever possible, including design of the business logo by Marcus and Ann's daughter Maddy. During the school holidays everyone took turns at trialling and developing recipes for sausage rolls and pasties.

Thanks to Amanda's Loddon Murray Community Leadership network, the Premier and Minister for Agriculture arrived for coffee and donuts during a mid-April tour of the district to announce drought funding. 'That was phenomenal,' she laughs, recalling the tweets put out over social media by Minister Jaala Pulford.

Locals are also heavily invested in the new bakery. The Pastor of Granite Church near Donald has created the legendary 'Broadway Challenge' on social media during his regular visits. 'He is eating his way through the pastry cabinet, one item at a time, and giving everyone a laugh in the process,' Amanda explains. Hmm. Sounds like I should plan a few more trips up the Calder if I'm going to keep up with the pastor. And I have since that very first interview.

Exciting news for Bakery on Broadway in 2020; the business is for sale! I caught up with Ann Durie and she explained that for various reasons the partners are now ready to pass the baton to new enthusiastic owners. 'We always had the intention of getting the business established and selling it on' – helped by the accurate books kept since the start so they can prove the business is a going concern and a solid investment. Good advice for any other business owner wanting to sell in the long term. There is no doubt that Bakery on Broadway has become an integral point of Wycheproof's central business district, giving travellers a reason to stop and spend their money.

During the first round of coronavirus restrictions the bakery was closed for eight weeks, with most staff able to receive JobKeeper support. 'Apart from a fortnightly bake for the locals, we scrubbed the bakery, repainted the tables and cleaned up around the place,' says Ann. 'We've had great help from our accountant and been well supported by the community since re-opening. It's nice to be back!'

So, what have I learnt from observing Bakery on Broadway over the years? They have proven that a group of people with a diverse range of skills and a vision to strengthen their community can make a start-up business not only achievable but a success.

Congratulations Wycheproof!

www.facebook.com/bakeryonbroadway

Royal Hotel Cooperative

Alison McClelland and John Clohesy, Royal Hotel

A local pub providing an important social meeting place is considered integral to every Australian town. In April 2017, when the Sea Lake Hotel burnt down and the only other pub in town was closed, action was clearly needed. Local resident, John 'Bull' Clohesy, picked up the phone and started calling a long list of people.

This wasn't the first time John, a local farmer, had helped to rally the locals. Significantly, one of the first people he called was Alison McClelland. She had been a key driver in forming the Sea Lake & District Hardware Cooperative two years earlier. 'She resisted at first,' John recalls with a chuckle, 'but now she's in, boots and all.'

Alison quietly smiles and the value of the partnership becomes apparent. While John has the passion and drive, Alison is one of those people who gets things done, including all the tedious paperwork.

With the success of the Hardware Cooperative behind them and the importance of retaining a social hub in their agricultural town with a population of 642, John was now pushing for a Royal Hotel Cooperative. In the lead up to the November 2018 auction 42 investors were secured, ensuring the somewhat dilapidated building, closed for the past 18 months, had a future.

'We set a $5000 minimum buy-in per share,' John explains, clarifying that regardless of how much they invested, each member only has one vote as per standard cooperative model rules. Significantly, many younger people in the district purchased shares in the Cooperative. 'It's filled a gap for the young ones and created a buzz about town,' John confirms. Six directors were appointed to the Cooperative, a mix of young and old.

With the Cooperative formed and the property purchased, they faced the biggest challenge, getting the 1910 building fit for purpose again. 'We took 28 truckloads of rubbish to the tip,' John recalls. 'Young and old worked together for seven months. Counting our volunteer contributions, we have invested $5 million so far.'

Local tradies and businesses including the Hardware Cooperative benefited along the way. Two local managers and weekly discussions kept everyone on track. Retaining as much of the historic charm as possible, the original floorboards now line a modern bar with a unique cement top, the brainchild of one of the Coop members and volunteer workers.

It was a proud moment for the whole town when the Royal Hotel reopened its doors on the long weekend in June 2019 with a fully refurbished bar, sports room, restaurant, ten accommodation rooms upstairs, and a beautiful veranda overlooking the main street.

In a stroke of genius (or just good luck!), a former Melbourne chef was coaxed to Sea Lake to establish 'The Juke' restaurant as a separate business within the Royal Hotel. 'Sixteen local jobs have been created,' John says with great satisfaction, glancing across at one of their young managers working behind the bar.

'None of us had hospitality experience,' Alison admits. 'We just opened the doors and winged it. So far, it's been successful, but we need to keep building capacity.' There are 20 more rooms behind the scenes awaiting refurbishment, so their task is not yet complete.

While the Royal Hotel's former patrons – local farmers and travelling harvest workers – would still clearly recognise their old pub, the refurbishment is now successfully meeting the needs of international and city tourists recently attracted to Sea Lake by the photogenic Lake Tyrrell and silo art trail. Thanks to the tenacity of the local community, it's a successful blend of old and new.

It's a busy week for Sea Lake and the Royal Hotel when I catch up with Alison McClelland in February 2020. 'Singles night is being held tomorrow night on the balcony for Valentine's Day,' she explains, reminding me there are many young farmers in the district looking for partners. They'd thrown around a few ideas of speed dating and their young manager took up the idea and ran with it. 'The ABC television crew are in town and the story is going to feature on Landline, which is terrific,' she tells me.

Having heard her partner in crime, John Clohesy, being interviewed on ABC Radio the previous week, it is obvious that the Royal Hotel story has captured everyone's imagination and given hope to other rural communities during a very tough time. 'The hotel has been going really well and we're getting contacted by a lot of other towns wanting to set up cooperatives. It's lovely we're getting the attention,' Alison agrees.

Three months later and it is a far different story thanks to coronavirus. The long weekend in June would have been the Royal Hotel's first birthday. Instead of celebrating, Alison admits to feeling stressed. 'We are trying to remain positive but are worrying about our financial solvency, like many other publicans from the area I've been speaking to.'

With crops successfully in the ground and no cases of COVID in the local area, we can only hope that this important community enterprise will bounce back in the coming months.

www.royalhotelsealake.com.au

Quambatook District Share Shop Inc

Jodie Russ (left) and fellow volunteers, Quambatook & Districts Share Shop Inc

Home-based businesses are gathering traction with their online retailing, but some customers want access to a physical storefront. Solving a problem for one such rural online business has resulted in a great outcome for the small town of Quambatook in the southern Mallee of Victoria.

Only a handful of businesses have survived in Quambatook (with its population of 249, Census 2016) and surrounding agricultural communities. So, it was with great celebration that the Quambatook & Districts Share Shop Inc. officially opened its doors on 11 January 2019.

It is a momentous day when I visit one month after opening. Sharing the retail space are 11 home-based businesses showing and selling their wares. If not for the Share Shop, they would find it difficult to get exposure for their products in a physical environment.

Thanks to the Quamby Silo Cinema screening of *The Merger* later in the day, there are people in town and a small but steady stream of customers. The Shop has also got its EFTPOS facilities up and running for the first time using a Square credit card reader. This may not seem like much until you understand where the Share Shop has come from and how far it still has to go. For starters, there is *no* power or running water to the building!

President of the Share Shop, Jodie Russ, recalls how she used to walk past the old store, its interior hidden by black plastic across the windows. Previously it had been home to Ellis's Hardware and Plumbing Supplies and Tom Hogan's Grocery Store. 'I moved to Quambatook 10 years ago and never knew what lay behind those blacked-out windows,' Jodie admits. 'It's always a shame to see old buildings unused.' So, when requests came from local and visiting customers to view Jodie's products from her online retail business, Retro Vintage Period, it was logical that she considered accessing a vacant storefront.

'I didn't really want people coming to my home,' she explains, 'but there was no way I could afford to open a store all by myself. I started thinking that perhaps there were others in similar circumstances. Or they had a hobby business that would benefit from more exposure.' Jodie points out that a lot of research and preparation went on before the Share Shop opened. A group of local people expressed their interest in the joint enterprise, including the owner of The Quambatook Stores who saw an opportunity to have her wares on sale over the weekend when she was closed for a much-needed rest.

Accessing a physical storefront turned out to be the easiest of all their tasks. Owner Graeme Elliott, who had inherited the old building, was only too willing to agree to a peppercorn lease to help the group get on their feet.

'I knocked on Graeme's door and he was marvellous,' Jodie recalls. 'He is so generous in supporting us for the first year to let us accumulate funds. The only stipulation was that we had to deal with what was behind the black plastic, which turned out to be lots of old engines and car parts.' A clearance sale was organised by a local auctioneer, and the majority of items were sold, clearing the way for the new occupants.

And the lack of power and water? 'We weren't going to let that stop us!' Jodie exclaims. 'We bring our own tank water in from home in buckets and have a gas ring to make a cuppa. And, on one of the hot days, the building owner hooked a car battery up to an inverter to run a fan for us.' As backup Jodie also purchased a second-hand generator from a Facebook Buy Swap Sell Site for $50. 'Of course, we'd love to have power,' Jodie admits, 'but it will cost us $25,000 to get all the wiring upgraded so that is a battle for another day.'

Settling on a legal and financial model for the group required further research but they realised that there was no need to reinvent the wheel. Assistance from the Gannawarra Shire and a minibus trip to speak with existing cooperative groups in the nearby towns of Sea Lake and Wycheproof enabled them to decide to become an incorporated entity. 'We have a yearly fee of $260 made up of $5 per week per business paid up front from 1 January, or pro rata on entry to 31 December,' explains Jodie, moving into business mode. 'Commission on goods sold is 10% if you volunteer your time to serve in the shop or 20% if you can't.'

While the overheads are minimal with no utilities connected, there is the peppercorn rent and insurance to be paid. 'The enterprise is committed to generating funds to enable it to effectively market the shop, pay rent and improve facilities in its second year of operation, and keep it rolling for years to come,' explains Jodie. For this reason, they have two fundraising coordinators as well as a treasurer. 'We need to build up our kitty and make this sustainable.'

Chatting with the team on duty, it is clear there are many benefits far beyond the opportunity to generate income for local businesses when the shop is open Friday, Saturday and Sundays. I'm particularly interested in Zoe, a Year 12 student. 'I'm just a floater,' she tells me. It turns out that Sue, her mother, is one of the Share Shop members and Zoe is fulfilling the volunteering component. Her current task is to write out the EFTPOS instructions for all the volunteers, which I'm sure will be gratefully received.

In fact, their very first EFTPOS sale takes place during our conversation to a couple from Portland in New South Wales who have been staying at the caravan park for the past week in eager anticipation of the silo cinema that evening. Another of their volunteer members, Fiona Williams, operates the EFTPOS and completes the sale, with guidance from Jodie. 'This is a wonderful opportunity to develop our technological skills,' Jodie points out as Fiona carefully watches the transaction go through their newly purchased mobile credit card reader.

Volunteer, Kathryn Robson

By default, the Share Shop has also become an important social hub to this small community and their secretary, Kathryn Robson, is a classic example. 'Fiona and I were wondering what we were doing in the early days,' Jodie admits, 'then Kathryn came and asked how she could help.' A district nurse by profession, Kathryn is a constant visitor to the store on her days off, bringing her unique enthusiasm, and what suspiciously appears to be a fetish for dressing up in the vintage clothing for their social media posts. During my visit she performs two super-fast clothing changes for the photographs.

'The flow-on effect of the Share Shop is immense,' Jodie says. 'It is so important for the town to have a drawcard and we can refer them to other businesses and places of interest. We took a gamble and it's paying off,' she concludes, looking around with a satisfied smile.

It's 2020, and a year of operation in the Quambatook District Share Shop. 'We had a thank you evening for our volunteers to keep the momentum up and make them feel appreciated, especially as the excitement of a new enterprise reduces over time.' Jodi reported a quiet summer but she was hoping business would build up again in the cooler months. 'Every event brings business to town. We've been averaging $2000 per month in sales, which is great when we only trade three days a week and five hours a day.' This enables the group to pay for its insurance and rate bills. Everything else is managed on a shoestring budget. 'It's all about the marketing, which is why I'm always putting up photos on social media,' Jodi adds. The group has attracted a new treasurer, 'a bookkeeper from Lake Boga I met at a workshop. I made sure I got his number!'

Jodi agrees that the Share Shop has provided many benefits for the people of Quambatook. 'It has brought a lot more skills and confidence to our volunteers, attributes they can use in their own lives and businesses.'

Like many other businesses, the Share Shop decided to close with coronavirus restrictions, but individuals continue to sell their wares online. They are looking forward to brighter times ahead.

www.facebook.com/quambatookdistrictshareshopinc

15 Acres

12-year-old Cooper Taylor, 15 Acres

We've heard the saying it takes a village to raise a child, however the Cohuna–Leitchville district in northern Victoria has taken it a step further. They are nurturing and encouraging young entrepreneurs!

It was a special day for the Taylor family at Leitchville. Not only was 14 January 2018 their pop's birthday, it was the launch of 12-year-old Cooper and 15-year-old Bailey Taylor's business, 15 Acres.

Their mother Kellie recalls the day Cooper came home and announced he had bought a business. 'You haven't,' was her reply. He had! And, after spending time with Cooper, I can understand how. This gregarious pre-teen doesn't lack in confidence; I have no doubt he could sell ice to the Eskimos if required.

Cooper had been earning pocket money by selling eggs from the 20 chooks he kept at his family home but it was proving to be problematic. In his words, 'people wanted heaps of eggs and I didn't have enough'. A 'mate' and advisor on a nearby property, who produced eggs on a much larger scale, was selling up. When Cooper was offered 160 chooks, two Maremma guard dogs and two caravans he had no hesitation in saying yes – which brings us back to his announcement to his parents. 'Well I haven't actually paid him yet,' admitted Cooper. 'But I will one day. He just wanted someone to love the chooks as much as he did. I don't like factory farms, that is my pet hate.'

At the same time his older brother Bailey had been seeking a part-time job, not easy when you live some distance from town and don't have a licence. This new business presented an opportunity for both brothers. It was then up to the boys to come to an agreement on what their responsibilities would be. 'Bailey isn't a morning person,' Cooper is quick to share. 'I do the morning chores and most of the infrastructure stuff.'

The more quietly spoken sibling Bailey explains that his role is to collect the eggs at night and look after the larger chooks and dogs. Cooper has been responsible for growing 200 chickens that are about to graduate to free range in the paddock. A bit of disagreement breaks into the conversation at this point. Cooper wants to dispute who is responsible for what. You know; that normal sibling stuff.

Quickly moving on I ask why they called their business 15 Acres? 'Well the previous business was called 400 Acres,' Cooper explains, successfully distracted. So, no need to ask how big their property is then!

Kept safe by the two Maremma dogs, Falcor and Jane, the chooks free range in the paddock while roosting and laying in caravans converted for

Bailey Taylor, 15 Acres

their exclusive use by the boys' grandpa. Various people around the district have donated a number of additional caravans. A heat lamp was also provided free of charge, and a local businessman has offered to build them a website. 'People are really nice and willing to help,' Cooper says. Everything he has learnt about caring for chooks and preparing eggs for market has been from his mate and from watching videos on YouTube. 'I haven't read any books,' Cooper admits.

It is approaching the end of the moulting season and there are fewer eggs to sell. Cooper admits this is a challenge; their customers include six local eateries and the Farmers & Made in Cohuna Market on the fourth Sunday of every month. 'We've been offered another caravan that we hope to use for the markets; we just need time to convert it,' Cooper says.

Time is a challenge, even for teenagers. 'I've got eight hours at school each day including bus travel, and I've got sport as well.' Cooper, due to leave for a football match playing for Leitchville Gunbower Under 12s, glances at the clock. Sport is extremely important in a rural community.

Let's talk money, I suggest, and ask Bailey if it has been worthwhile. 'I'm glad that I got involved,' he says. 'It's going well at the moment and we should do well in the future as the layers pick up.' Usually on a Sunday the boys convene at the kitchen table to assess their cash flow. The profits are split while leaving a set amount in kitty to cover change and feed costs.

At this point Cooper cuts in to accuse his mother of helping herself to a bit of petty cash on a few occasions. 'She treats it as an ATM,' he claims. This argument falls flat when I ask how much they pay her to cover the transport expenses of delivering the eggs, going to the markets, and collecting the chook feed supplies – 66 cents per kilometre is the going rate I helpfully point out as Kellie chuckles in the background. Cooper is momentarily silent.

With another successful diversion in place I wonder how they established their retail price? 'We started at $5 per dozen but put it up to $6 for the market,' Cooper bounces back. He is clear on what their expenses are. 'It costs $450 to fill the big container,' he explains. 'If we bought 20 kilo bags it would cost a lot more so we buy in bulk, which reduces the cost per kilo.'

Kellie helped the boys to establish a business page on Facebook and a business card; however, it seems that word of mouth is pretty much doing the job for them. It is clear to me that everyone in the district is keen to nurture more young people to experience and develop business skills, and these two enterprising brothers are only too happy to take up the challenge.

School resumed in February 2020, and the Cohuna Farmer's Market was continuing to bring in good sales for the boys. All was looking rosy, with 60 dozen eggs sold on 27 January! Business was so good they'd become a sponsor of the Black Swan Creek Marathon.

In April came the sad announcement on their Facebook page that a decision had been made to close down the business because of the uncertainty around coronavirus and the social isolation. Cooper found a few cows to fill in this time. 'I think it was the right decision,' says Cooper, 'but we're thinking about going back into it soon.' You can't keep a good entrepreneur down!

www.facebook.com/15-Acres-893893514125933

AMPLIFTS

Brendan Murphy, AMPLIFTS (photo supplied)

Brendan Murphy, just 18 years of age and living in the tiny town of Allanson in south-west Western Australia, was midway through Year 12 at nearby Collie Senior High School in 2018 – when he launched his first business!

When the school bell rings Brendan is the first one out the door to catch the bus home. But instead of sitting and watching television or playing the video games he used to be addicted to, he is rushing home to work on his online fitness program and coaching business at AMPLIFTS.com

In collaboration with Adam Peeler, a young fitness fanatic in the United States, Brendan has capitalised on modern technology to create a passive income, before he has even left school. I'm impressed when I check out the website. The technology is good, the copy snappy, and both Brendan and Adam present themselves professionally. 'It has been hard to find the time to work on the business,' Brendan admits, 'but I made a lot of progress during the school holidays.'

But how did he learn how to do all this? 'The content is based on maximising my own results,' explains Brendan. 'I got involved in fitness, bodybuilding and powerlifting and studied the science behind it.' Adam, who has a major in exercise science, became one of Brendan's trusted sources as he scoured the internet for articles and tutorials.

After messaging Adam via a Facebook community, the two hit it off immediately and a business partnership was formed. 'Adam was already a big name in the industry in the United States so it was good to have his endorsement and for him to be part of the business. A lot of people claim to know everything but can't back up what they say with facts,' says Brendan. 'What we follow is the science behind training and nutrition and strive to apply that when we create programs for natural lifters who aren't on steroids.'

With the business still in its infancy they are only just starting to make money. There's an agreed 40/60 split of the profits, with the majority going to Brendan who looks after the website. With the benefits of digital technology, and having worked out the time differences between Collie and Utah, they converse daily via Facebook messenger.

Brendan and Adam provide testimonials that would most appeal to their primary audience, young men. Both talk about how they transitioned from insecure young men into confident ones through their fitness regimes, and they aren't afraid of sharing positive stories about self-esteem and mental health via social media and YouTube. They've also showcased the incredible results their clients have achieved through the use of their programs on the website.

When it came to establishing a website Brendan did what every wise businessperson should do. He invested in Squarespace, a well-known software platform, and customised it for a fresh look. He also checked out competitor websites. 'I took what they do and did it better. It was important for my website to be user friendly; some are just too confusing.' Having an interest in web development and coding – self-taught of course – he found it an easy task.

As an online business, AMPLIFTS' customers can be located anywhere in the world. Capitalising on their social media presence, marketing so far has been via Facebook and Instagram plus Google advertisements. 'We've been getting three to five per cent click through on our adverts but the challenge is to convert them into sales,' Brendan says.

Recently AMPLIFTS received a welcome boost when Adam stayed with a popular YouTuber in the United States who has more than 100,000 followers. 'We received a few sales out of that,' Brendan notes gratefully.

When time permits Brendan is looking forward to developing an app so their customers can access their programs offline and track their progress. In the meantime, there is school, I remind him cheerfully. 'Yeah ...' he acknowledges. When asked why he is doing Year 12 he admits that it is to get an ATAR score and, I assume, to meet university admission requirements. However, Brendan is quick to assure me that university is not his intended future. 'I will be working AMPLIFTS full time and hopefully collaborating with Adam in person in the United States,' he says with much more enthusiasm.

Two years later and much has changed. The partnership with Adam has ended. Brendan has retained a few clients to coach and expanded his work to graphic and web design. His heart is still set on building a business around his passion. 'I have a powerlifting competition in three months, where I am aiming to be the best in Australia this year for my age and weight class,' he says. Prior to coronavirus he was also training twice a week with the Hands of Steel Arm Wrestling Club in Bunbury.

'If I can gain a bigger name in the powerlifting world my goal is to open a new business purely focused on training strength athletes online. Perhaps I will own a gym, too, and a supplement company,' he muses. Wisely, Brendan is hedging his bets. 'I plan to spend more time learning about the Foreign Exchange market and pursue that professionally, too.'

Whatever he ends up doing he is continuing to learn valuable business skills along the way.

Business Reflections

Over the past five years I've interviewed hundreds of rural businesspeople. Nothing can beat a lived and authentic business story, but I also pay close attention to worldwide trends through online articles and at the various events and forums I attend. We are indeed fortunate that we live in a world where so much information is at our fingertips. So many people have such valuable information to share.

Quite often the ideas and business tips put forward contradict each other. One businessperson told me, 'Fake it until you make it,' while another said, 'Be honest about what you can do.' Our role is to provide ideas and share what did and didn't work for us. As someone who is in the unique position of having been in business, and is now talking to people in a wide variety of businesses operating in a rapidly changing world, I appreciate that we all have to make the best decision for our own situation and at that particular moment in time.

Sometimes ideas work and sometimes they don't. But the learning is always powerful and opens up new opportunities further down the track. There is no rule book to follow. Entrepreneurship can be referred to as a combination of art and science incorporating all the 10 characteristics or attributes I've profiled in previous chapters.

I've written some thought pieces that may also be of interest to you, like joining the dots from lots of different conversations and my own experiences. It's not rocket science by any means, but it is important. We need to value what we are doing and become ambassadors for each other. Practical tips on topics such as finance can be helpful to those just starting up. Some of my articles, for instance, *Value Yourself*, have resonated strongly with small businesses and trended on national media.

A lot of this is common sense. Occasionally, however, we need a reminder of how amazing we are, why we should value ourselves, and how we can keep improving our businesses by working together and sharing ideas.

Erasing Normal, the first article here, was written shortly after the start of COVID-19 and the restrictions being placed on businesses across Australia in March 2020. The second, *How Future Proof Is Your Business?*, was written two years earlier. Both emphasise that we can never be complacent in this rapidly changing world. We all need to continually innovate.

Erasing 'normal'

Kerry's advice to rural businesses when COVID-19 restrictions were introduced

As the brutal bushfires of the 2019–20 summer were quelled, rural businesses across Australia breathed a sigh of relief and began planning for a more positive year ahead. Then a virus from overseas entered our shores and the rest is history.

COVID-19 has affected businesses in multiple ways with uncertainty being a common denominator. What has been most heartening is seeing new ways of thinking and doing business emerging. Quite literally, it has taken a pandemic to shake us out of our complacency and it is the most adaptable, innovative and collaborative who thrive. Why would we want to return to 'normal'?

The impact of COVID-19 on businesses has varied. Some have closed their doors temporarily and for those that were marginal to begin with, there will be no appetite for a comeback. Many have limped along in a limited capacity to try and meet overheads. For the lucky ones it is business *almost* as usual, and others are stretched to capacity to meet demand. While some feel guilty that they are able to continue operating when so many have been forced to close, I believe they should instead feel grateful. No business is an island. We are all in this together and your success is our success.

Regardless of what situation your business is in, we have one thing in common. We have all had to deal with uncertainty, and the inevitable stress. Now is a good time to stop and enquire how your fellow business owners are going. Despite bravado they will be hurting in some way. Just showing that you care and understand will help them and it may well be beneficial for you both.

Let us be under no illusion. This will be a long recovery process for those most impacted and professional assistance should be sought to plan ahead. We need to start looking forward but, in the rush to get back to 'normal', we would be doing ourselves a great disservice not to think about the good things that have emerged during the coronavirus restrictions.

Use of online technology

First and foremost, there has been a huge uptake in the use of online technology for communication and reaching new markets. So much dead travel time has been saved and rural businesses that have been struggling to survive on local or tourist trade have been reminded that there is a world out there. The goodwill has never been higher to support rural and family operated businesses providing we offer customers online options.

Diversification

Those businesses who have been most affected have used the time to explore how they can diversify their offer and their markets. Existing equipment and skills have been pivoted to filling gaps in the supply chain and producing new products such as hand sanitiser. New skills have been learnt and are in the process of being applied to new business products and services.

New processes

Remote work and improved hygiene practices for staff and customers have been a major focus of those still able to operate. Communication aims to instil customers with confidence that we can still safely do business, and to advise of any changes in the way services are being provided. We've learnt that it's not enough to just *do* it, we have to demonstrate we are doing it.

Collaboration

As supply chains have been stressed, new ways of doing business have been thrust upon us, and businesses have considered how they can support each other. Simple things like sharing transport and supplies or promoting a small business's products on another business's website are truly heartening. We are so much stronger when we work together, share costs, and promote each other.

Work / Life Balance

For busy business owners, the pandemic restrictions on socialising have reminded us of the importance of family. For those who have been restricted in our business operations, it has given us the opportunity work on our business and our personal wellbeing. This has been a valuable time to assess how we can balance our time more effectively.

Should we stop doing any of this? Definitely not!

It has taken a pandemic to shake us out of our complacency and it is the most adaptable who thrive. Let us continue to embrace change through ongoing collaboration and innovation.

How futureproof is your business?

Apple co-founder Steve Wozniak at the 2017 Pivot Summit in Geelong

Sitting in a predominantly young audience at a Pivot Summit held in Geelong in 2017, it suddenly occurred to me that this generation has no conception of a world pre-computers and the internet.

We were listening to Apple co-founder Steve Wozniak's reminiscences of building a computer from scratch because to buy one was the equivalent to the cost of a house in the 1970s. Who would have thought that today we would have access to a mini computer courtesy of our smart phone! In fact, who would have thought we'd be carrying our own personal phone not connected by wire to a wall?

Times are changing so rapidly in this digital and technological age. Every decade sees major innovation. Not only new products being invented but the way we work and do everyday tasks is changing.

With the acceleration of driverless cars on to the market, there is a strong chance that the toddlers in our families will never need a driver's licence. Instead there will be a market for recreational driving tracks, similar to riding schools for horses. And cars will be fitted out with beds and luxury screens as customers book an overnight ride from Melbourne to Sydney. Concert tickets may include a pick-up service. The list is endless for discerning businesspeople.

Which brings me to the question. How futureproof is your business? If we don't ask that question, there is potential for looming disaster. I see it time and time again. Disgruntled business owners closing their doors because they have kept doing the same old thing and wondering why their customers were disappearing.

In my experience there are three good reasons for innovating your business: growing profits, increasing safety and efficiency, and staying relevant. If you don't offer that new experience, product or service to your customers, someone else will.

It makes good sense to keep an eye on new trends and to give yourself the space to think creatively. For some this comes naturally, for others it is a foreign language. How can we get ourselves into this headspace?

The gurus tell us that we should be reading a new book each week. Hmm. Well at least follow some interesting blogs on social media that you can skip through over a coffee. As painful as it may be to take time out of the business, it is important to sign up for at least one interesting business-related event each year. Choose something different. Even an online webinar with an obscure title! For some a personal business coach may be the answer but it will depend on the quality of that coach as to the results you will get.

Some of the greatest insights come from everyday conversations and observations. The idea for a McDonald's drive through came from a bank installing a drive through night safe for its business customers.

My advice is to tear yourself away from your usual peer group. Always be curious and make new conversations.

Think like a start-up

Building a successful business takes a lot of blood, sweat and tears. Sometimes it can take up to five years and longer to get established, but every savvy business owner understands that you can never truly get comfortable. Complacency is our biggest enemy and it pays to think like a start-up on a regular basis.

In a rapidly changing environment, here are six questions that can help keep your business fresh and viable.

1# Is the business profitable?

Unless this is an expensive hobby, then this is the priority question. If the answer is no, and you don't know why, then you need to explore the next five questions even more closely.

#2 Do I have adequate skills and resources to meet current and future needs?

What can be outsourced, what needs to be provided in-house? Lease versus capital purchases? There are lots of options that can ease you through times of consolidation and/or growth. Don't be afraid to seek professional assistance whether it be for business planning or logistics. And don't forget to consider collaborating with fellow businesses to help share costs.

#3 Am I happy in my business?

If going to work each day is a chore, we have to ask ourselves why. Do I need a break? Do I need assistance? Do I need a new challenge? Is it because our business is struggling? If the latter, we need to understand why it is struggling. Option A is to do something about it. Option B is to exit the business as quickly as possible.

#4 Are staff happy in their work?

We also need to ask these same questions of our staff in a way they are prepared to answer honestly. Unhappy staff may come as a complete surprise if left to fester and ultimately can impact significantly on the business.

#5 Is the business still relevant in what it provides?

Are sales going up or down and in which particular products and/or services? Demand may still be strong but with nuances. It pays to keep an eye on what is happening globally so there are no nasty surprises. And don't forget to keep asking your customers: Are we providing exactly what you are looking for?

#6 Is the business still relevant in the way it services customers?

Disruption is here to stay. Fifty years ago, disruption came in the form of self-service supermarkets and drive-through fast food. Now, in the digital age, the way we service our customers is constantly changing and new products and services beyond our previous imagination are emerging *every* day.

And a few final words of advice. Don't toss the baby out with the bathwater! What do your customers appreciate about your business? Keep doing it! What else would they appreciate? Start doing it!

Be loud and proud

'Being successful in business is my greatest contribution to the community.' **Tom Smith**

My journey to talk up business and publish a book began in 2010 when I accompanied a group of young farmers on a road tour to amazing places to meet amazing people. I introduced them to Tom Smith, a pork grower from Yarrawalla in north-west Victoria, and asked Tom what I thought was a straightforward question. His response was surprising.

Knowing of his long-term community work, I asked Tom what he considered to be his most valuable contribution to the community. His simple clear answer has stayed with me to this day. 'Being successful in business is my greatest contribution,' Tom replied. He explained that by being successful in business he was able to employ more than 30 people, which allowed them and their families to live in the region, attend the local schools, and benefit the community in so many different ways. His businesses have continued to grow and now employ more than 40 people. The nearby town of Pyramid Hill relies on his workers for the school and supermarket to remain open.

Since listening to Tom, I've become more aware of just how negative our society is about business and how little we understand the important role that business plays in our wellbeing overall. 'Big business' is deemed 'greedy' and 'unethical' in the media – often without basis or analysis. Those enjoying success can be subject to the 'tall poppy syndrome' treatment. 'Social enterprise' has become the preferred choice of terminology, almost as if an apology for it being a business. None of this reflects all the wonderful business people I know who do so much for their communities.

Tom opened my eyes to why a healthy business sector should be a priority of every Australian, regardless of whether they reside in a rural town or a large city. When appreciating why entrepreneurs and business in general are so important, it comes down to two factors. The first is that we can't all be employees, otherwise who would employ us? The second is that we need a majority of our population contributing revenue through the tax system to provide all those essential government services, such as health, education and welfare, that our growing population relies on.

With baby boomers reaching retirement age we are fast approaching a catastrophic imbalance, with far less revenue being contributed to support a growing population. Underpinning our country's health and wellbeing is the opportunity for the majority of our population to be gainfully employed. This is where the business sector plays an important role.

The CSRIO's 2016 'Tomorrow's Digitally Enabled Workforce' heralded the next 20 years as the era of the entrepreneur. We can only hope that many more will take up the challenge. So, my advice is to be loud and proud if you are successful in business and know that by doing so you are helping your community.

KERRY'S TIPS:

- Get over the tall poppy syndrome
  While we adore our winners on the sporting field and love it when an underdog performs well, why is it different when someone is successful in business? Their success is good for us all.

- Celebrate failure
  Repeat after me: It's ok to make mistakes! Just read the biography of any famous entrepreneur or inventor, every failure is a step closer to success. Sadly, instead of recognising their courage and tenacity, we tend to ridicule those who falter.

- Correct false perceptions
  Perceptions can be both powerful and wrong. Remind your customers and community about how much you contribute just by being in business.

No business is an island

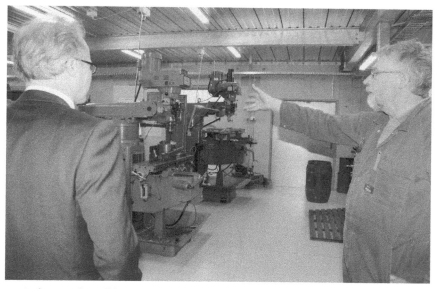

A cluster of small businesses has developed around the specialist automotive industry in Castlemaine

When I was judging a regional business awards some years ago, a business owner made a remark during an interview that has stuck with me. He said: 'No business is an island; we all have to work together.'

In a highly competitive world, it was refreshing to hear this perspective. In this instance the owner of the restaurant recognised the benefit for them of their town street prospering and attracting more customers. You could be the best restaurant in Australia but if the surrounding shops are closed or shabby it reflects badly, and customers are likely to keep driving.

But what about if another restaurant opens right next door? Bring it on I say! For a start, competition is healthy. It keeps you thinking about how to do things better. It also gives you the opportunity to create points of differences so you can cater for a wide range of tastes. And, when you're booked out, you can refer on!

In another rural Victorian town, the proprietor of an antique and collectibles store was absolutely delighted when two more identical businesses opened up right next door. 'It gives customers more of a reason to visit,' she explained. 'Knowing there are a number of antique and collective shops to browse, we become a drive-to destination.'

This is equally true of my hometown, which has built up an impressive specialist automotive industry over a 30-year period. What started as a hobby for a group of street rodding enthusiasts is now a cluster of complementary businesses, each catering for a different need. From restoration to auto electrics and panel beating, your needs will be met; our rural town has effectively become a one-stop shop. As a result, hundreds of people visit each week, as customers *and* tourists. When an event is held the numbers can be in the thousands, benefitting just about every business in town.

Every community needs a mix of businesses to ensure that customers are catered for locally and don't go elsewhere. It can be tough to get started and stay in business, so we business owners need to help each other. An encouraging word, some friendly advice, and participation in collaborative marketing opportunities can help our businesses grow together.

As the award-winning business owner said, 'No business is an island.'

Creating value

Every business needs to earn more than it spends, preferably resulting in a profit. And yet, when I talk to entrepreneurs and businesspeople around rural Australia, rarely is money their incentive to go into business. It is more likely to be a need to solve a problem, to fill a gap, or to simply create their own income so they can live and work where they want.

In a recent article, Johannes Larsson, an online entrepreneur living the high life on a healthy passive income, confirms that business success is not achieved by focusing on money. He openly admits that he started creating business ideas for the sole purpose of making big money. He failed. Repeatedly. It took seven years before he found success with financer.com. 'Ironically, I only began to see results in my business when I shifted my focus from trying to make money to creating value by providing people with a useful service,' Johannes admitted during this revealing interview with Celinne Da Costa.

However, as a business grows and staff are employed, life becomes more complicated. A current trend I am seeing, particularly with the trades, is to appoint a business manager. On the surface it seems like a great idea; to let the owner and qualified tradies get on with the job and clocking up billable hours. In theory a good business manager will seek to maximise revenue, yet I am observing all too many cases where inexperienced managers are focused on reducing costs. The consequences can be dire. The good employees leave and, most significantly, the bad ones stay. Not good for business! Do these business managers understand the cost of orientating a new employee and the potential damage to customer relationships? On the bright side, former employees often become sub-contractors to other businesses with the capacity to earn more income.

As future trends have predicted, the corporate world is also moving away from an employee model to that of sub-contracting work out, requiring more people to be self-employed. More recently, coronavirus has highlighted how people can successfully work remotely. This is great news for regional Australia as many start to consider the benefits of rural life and exit our smog-ridden, traffic-clogged, expensive cities.

Which brings me back to the article that caught my eye. Johannes says that his second biggest realisation was that having employees in a 9 to 5 office structure was defeating the point of making money online, i.e. having freedom and location independence. He let his employees go and switched to the 'intrapreneur model' – which means people work as entrepreneurs inside of the business – to ensure everyone is as motivated and driven as he is.

Those who work on a sub-contract basis can potentially have a more flexible lifestyle and be rewarded according to their efforts, a win-win for all concerned.

Value yourself

Like most small business owners in a rural community, you try to please your customers by offering a reasonable price for your goods and services. We may even drop that reasonable price lower again for a 'nice' local who reveals how tough they are doing it. They work for a set salary while struggling to raise a family. You know them well because your kids go to school with theirs.

Over the years this 'nice' local becomes a loyal customer as they work hard to improve their situation and, true to form, each time they cite tough times as they send their children to university, renovate their family home, and then move to a new location and build a new home. In return for their loyalty and in sympathy, you continue to cut a bit off your invoice.

Fast forward 25 years and that 'nice' local has retired with their healthy superannuation to enjoy that new holiday home and top model 4WD just purchased with 'their' hard-earned savings. You look at your books and wonder how you're ever going to retire, let alone trade in the work vehicle that should have been replaced five years ago.

Two questions came to mind when I heard this sadly true and all-too-common story. How highly do your customers value and respect your business? More importantly, how highly do you value and respect yourself?

While you provide a high-quality service or product to maintain your integrity and reputation in a small community, dropping your price doesn't necessarily increase customer satisfaction. They will still complain just as heartily; probably more so because their respect for you is already low. And they will continue to expect low prices *every* time. And, let's be clear, *you* gave them permission to think and behave this way.

So, what can we do differently as a small business owner?

- Understand your worth and respect your right to earn a decent living.
- Be clear on your product or service's true value. If compared with a cheaper alternative make sure that customers understand the differences in quality, transport costs, and access to follow-up service.
- Only discount when it is strategic, and it doesn't impact on your bottom line.
- Offer alternatives such as lay-by and part payments when a customer cites difficulty.
- Walk away when you need to.
- Look after yourself so you can then look after others.

Entrepreneurial learning

Entrepreneurs are learning no matter what they're doing!

At a conference I was once asked where entrepreneurs in rural areas go for learning and support. It was a great question, one that I have thought about while interviewing various entrepreneurs over a number of years. The answer is not straightforward because there is no one place to go.

Entrepreneurs are driven to solve a problem or take advantage of an opportunity. In order to do this, they tap into every resource they can find and need at that particular time. Then they move on because there is always a new challenge on the horizon and new things to learn when you are an entrepreneur.

While chambers of commerce, progress associations, and co-working spaces strive to be a hub for entrepreneurs they will never realistically meet all their needs. Don't get me wrong; I am a great supporter of these organisations, they play an important role in supporting business growth. Entrepreneurs, however, are quite different to the majority of those in business. Yes, in the early days of their business, entrepreneurs will take advantage of the networking and the speakers and workshops. They will then move to higher levels of networking and exploration with fellow entrepreneurs nationally and globally.

At the 2018 International Rural Women's Day event I hosted in Boort, the speakers jumped at the opportunity to have a road trip together. While happy to donate their time to encourage other women to enter the business world, they clearly recognised the value of learning from each other. We had three hours of incredible conversation in the car and my only regret is I didn't record it! As MC at the previous year's event, I had to step in to remind our panel of incredible female entrepreneurs of their audience as they became engrossed in their own conversation.

And so much learning these days is available to us online. Google and assess; move on. In fact, it is the entrepreneurs who are creating much of the Google content as they forge new frontiers and overcome barriers.

Entrepreneurs will learn something new while buying a loaf of bread. They are highly curious and continually observing what is happening around them and asking questions of complete strangers. They know no boundaries and visibly chafe at the constraints of formal learning channels. That is why we need to create different networking opportunities in interesting places. It is also why we need to freely share information and support others in their quests, even if we don't quite understand what they are striving for.

Overcoming financial barriers

Starting up or purchasing a business in a rural community has its advantages. Residents of a rural town will be your ambassadors, customers, and potentially your investors.

Start-up costs of a business may appear overwhelming. There is the purchase or lease of a workplace and equipment, purchase of stock, payment of staff, marketing costs plus legal and insurance fees. Then your bank, the one that gave you a home loan without a second thought, proves not so accommodating.

Passion and commitment, backed up by solid business planning, can overcome financial barriers. Here are some alternatives to explore.

Loans: From my experience in small businesses, a personal loan is often provided by a family member, or they act as guarantor for a commercial loan. It could even be a silent investor living in your community who sees it as a solid return. Either way, have a written agreement or legal contract. There is no better way to ruin a friendship or family relationship, especially when a sibling or partner weighs into the conversation at a later date.

Buying-in: The goodwill, stock, plant and equipment, and freehold of a business can potentially be made in separate payments over time, reducing the burden. For instance, a building could be leased for a period of time with option to buy. I've also heard of the new owner paying for stock as it is sold. Of course, this will only occur when there is trust between the buyer and seller. Many family businesses transfer ownership over a period of time, often in salary-sacrificing style. It can also be financially lucrative for the seller, as Vets All Natural discovered. They profited from the increased sales generated by the new buyer. A win-win situation.

Advance sales: A reduced price offer on membership to a gymnasium or specials on treatments purchased before opening day can be effective. A similar concept is crowd funding, where customers pre-purchase a product, effectively paying in advance for its production.

Partnerships: Sharing the risk and investment with others makes sense but potentially can be fraught with difficulties if you don't find people who share your passion and vision. A partner could be a spouse or another businessperson bringing capital, skills, or their existing client base into the mix. On a larger scale it could be a public company or a cooperative, which are common in rural areas. Community goodwill is a key driver of a cooperative, created when a service is under threat, such as a general store in a small town. Shares raise finance and the members are responsible to run the enterprise. Maximising profits of a group of primary producers by pooling resources for economy of scale is another common motive.

Whatever method you choose to finance your new business, make sure it is carefully thought through with a legal structure and clearly documented expectations to support it.

Local government planning

When Darren Fuzzard was appointed CEO of the Mount Alexander Shire in 2016, he agreed to meet with business owners to learn more about issues relating to local government

Opening or extending a business should be cause for community-wide celebration, but sadly is often marred by the frustration of dealing with local government. It appears this is not an isolated incidence, particularly for those converting existing buildings to a new purpose.

Clearly the fault does not lie solely with local government. Not only are councils being asked to regulate higher building standards, policy is forcing them to be more risk averse. But could they do it better? I believe improvement could be made by all of us.

From a business perspective it is wise to do your homework before you start. Even then allow a contingency in your project plans for hidden costs and unexpected delays. In one instance a group of business partners diligently researched other rural bakeries in preparation for their new start-up. While allowing for the installation of disability access and modernisation of the premises they didn't realise that even more stringent regulations apply to a building that changes purpose of business. This impacted on both their budget and their opening date. Ouch! At the other end of the spectrum a business owner suffered a lengthy application process only to discover that he hadn't been required to do so. Double ouch!

Interpretation of 'one-size-fits-all' regulations and a lack of common sense is a huge area of concern for small businesses in a rural setting. A niche butter factory that relocated in order to expand was stunned to be told that a proposed car park would need to be sealed, a cost they hadn't considered in a rural context and beyond their already stretched budget. Ideally these extra requirements could be staged or enforced at a later date when considered necessary.

Delays in inspections and issuing of permits is a common complaint. While a business owner is counting the cost of mounting finance and lost potential income, council staff and contractors may only be allocated to this role on certain days and not replaced when on leave.

Keep an accurate record of all correspondence and conversations. One businesswoman resorted to visiting the council each week to try and progress her permit application and constantly received different responses from different staff members.

Know your rights. If council doesn't respond within a certain time (eg. after 60 days in Victoria) you can take the issue to tribunal; however, be warned that any request by council for more information can potentially reset this time frame.

For all these reasons some businesses are engaging private town planners, a wise investment if you don't have the time and patience to deal with bureaucracy. And keep in mind, council has all the power so there is no point going on the attack. A good way forward is to make sure you keep your end of the bargain and negotiate common sense compromises where possible. Keep your cool and communicate! Forge closer relationships; invite council staff to visit your business. In the meantime, small business needs to keep lobbying government for more flexibility and increased access to council services.

Cooperatives

The Culgoa Store is just one of many cooperatives operating in rural towns

Over the years everything from a rural general store to the local pub or hardware store has closed its doors, only to be re-opened as a cooperative. Essentially a cooperative fills a gap, providing goods or services the community feels are integral to their continued success and wellbeing. However, there is also a second and equally important objective of a cooperative, and that is to make a profit.

It is far simpler to form a company than a cooperative I discovered when chatting to a few people involved in rural cooperatives. Making a profit can also be a challenge. Kerri Barry has been a director of the Culgoa Community Co-operative since it first formed in 2003. 'Pick a year, there is always some crisis happening, but in 2000 it was two-fold. We had a drought and our only shop was closing.'

Starting a cooperative doesn't happen overnight. Over the past 30 years GMG Financial Group, based in Swan Hill, Charlton and Balranald, has assisted coops to get started in the region and, according to managing partner Rick Pickering, it is a long process. In many ways determining whether a cooperative is the best path to take is the easiest part. 'While a company structure is better suited to four or five partners, a cooperative is a far better vehicle if you wish to have varying share structures for a large number of shareholders,' says Rick.

Legislation in each State requires that you first hold a public meeting to determine if there is sufficient interest before forming a steering committee to establish what kind of model rules you wish to adopt. Fortunately, in the case of Culgoa, population 339, there was immediate general consensus, says Kerri. 'We all knew how important the store was to our community's mental health. If our store went it would tip us over the edge. The owner had bad health and couldn't sell the business. It was the only solution to maintain this service in town.'

In October 2015, a cooperative was formed in nearby Sea Lake to re-open their local hardware store and avoid a gap in their local retail sector. An impressive 100 people out of a population of 616 attended the initial public meeting. Having a key driver who is respected in the community and a group of supporting champions is essential to get a cooperative up and running. In Sea Lake, a concerned farmer who had the experience of being a grain cooperative shareholder generated interest. He convinced other key people in the community to get on board.

'We then ran a campaign to get the whole community interested,' explains Alison McClelland, who was subsequently elected secretary of the Sea Lake & District Co-operative Ltd. 'Our aim was to not lose another business and keep people shopping in Sea Lake. We wrote articles for the local newspaper and rang people. Once a steering committee is formed their first decision is to decide on what model rules to adopt and, depending on the level of expertise available to you, this may involve communicating with professionals,' says Rick, who became involved with Sea Lake right from the start.

'A submission to the Department of Fair Trading that governs cooperatives in Victoria is akin to writing a feasibility study,' he explains. 'A business model needs to cover membership, share capital, the type of business being conducted, directors and cash flow budget. Essentially you need to think right through the process when deciding on model rules.'

'We gathered expressions of interest and kept everyone informed through the newspaper and by email,' says Alison. 'At our second meeting we started outlining our proposed level of investment. A starting base of $5000 was out of some people's reach but they still wanted to be involved. For this reason, we dropped it to $2000 and basically accepted anything over $1000.'

Most of the work was done by volunteers in Culgoa, setting up the cooperative and getting the store up and running. 'It was a lot of work filling out the application,' concedes Kerri who did the bulk of the work when it was under the jurisdiction of Consumer Affairs Victoria. 'The trick is to find one person in the Department you can deal with.' Under current legislation, once a cooperative's application meets compliance the model rules are presented at a 'Formation Meeting' with a formal motion to form a cooperative.

Ultimately Sea Lake raised $200,000 through 60 shareholders. 'We would have liked more but it was enough to open the doors in February 2016,' says Alison. 'Originally we had an agreement to rent the building for five years but then that changed to having to buy it with a few of us agreeing to be guarantors for a loan. It also took a lot of money to stock the shelves. We have a five-year plan and are very mindful we have a mortgage hanging over our heads.'

Over a decade earlier, the Culgoa Co-operative received the bonus of federal funding to purchase the store and refurbish it at a modest cost. Shareholders then purchased a minimum of 50 shares at $1 each. 'Cooperatives can attract funding,' says Kerri. 'We also had 12 months of wages covered but it was always our intention to run the store on a volunteer basis. It was a great honeymoon period but then, because of the drought, people involved in the shop had to go and get paid work which affected our volunteer base.'

'Ultimately any cooperative must seek to make a profit so they can be distributed back to members,' says Rick. 'For example, you can pay a dividend based on how many shares you own or you could pay a rebate or bonus based on how much business a shareholder does with the cooperative rather than their number of shares.' He points out that accounting processes in a cooperative are the same as for any small business but the reality, as we all know, can often be quite different with cooperatives sometimes just striving to survive.

'If it had been a private business it would have been closed long ago,' Kerri says of the Culgoa Community Store. 'But because we've put our own money in, we all make sure it stays open. We are diligent in making sure we are in a position where we can pay our bills and sometimes have to fundraise.'

Governance can also be fraught with difficulties as people come and go. In a cooperative every shareholder has an equal vote, regardless of how many shares they hold. Some people put in more time than others, some are more highly skilled, and everyone brings different personalities to the table.

'As a board we are required to meet a minimum of four times a year,' says Kerri, 'but we find it's best to meet more regularly to be on top of things and have clear communication. In a small community, it is sometimes hard to separate our board role from being a volunteer.'

'There are varying levels of professionalism in cooperatives,' says Rick. 'If you have a good committee and treasurer, then generally a cooperative can cope, but if there is a change of personnel suddenly, they might not be running so well.'

'We didn't realise the financial strain and the workload of keeping the paperwork in order,' admits Kerri. 'In hindsight we would have just had one person doing the accounting side of it.'

A lot has also changed in the 13 years since Culgoa was established, some good, some bad. One recent change for the better is that coops are no longer required to be audited as long as they continue to meet their model rule requirements. This news was met with great delight in Culgoa where they had struggled with this financial burden in their initial years.

'A new challenge,' says Kerri, 'is that our population has shrunk and sometimes we find it difficult to get five directors and they can't always be involved hands-on. The re-start and traineeship employment programs have enabled us to employ some part-time staff but a few times we've had to have the hard conversation of whether to close or to put in more volunteer hours. Each time the community rallies but we are only just making ends meet.'

The Sea Lake community has required a much larger financial contribution for their venture. 'We are conscious that people have invested their own money and it is important to run a good business,' says Alison. 'For this reason, we got good back up from an accountant right from the beginning and this cost is built into our annual budget.'

Trying to find the right people to work in the business is another challenge. 'We are learning skills as we go. We started off with just a cash register and no EFTPOS, which we've since discovered is essential for stock control. There is so much work behind the scenes setting up computers.'

The Sea Lake Hardware Co-operative continues to successfully operate since opening in 2015

A paid manager has been appointed, but Alison is still a hands-on volunteer doing a bit of everything while the store gets established. Shareholders pitched in to get the store open and continue to help out when they can. Exploring ways of running a cooperative more efficiently is obviously a smart move. Culgoa has picked up the local postal service while Sea Lake is keen to diversify in the future. 'We should be looking at employment incentives, traineeships and work experience options as well,' says Alison, but admits they have been just too busy.

All difficulties aside, there have been no regrets for those involved in either of these two rural cooperatives. 'Even if we had known all this in hindsight, we still had the drive and passion,' says Kerri.

'It's all about community involvement,' says Alison. 'We might not be making millions but we're holding our own and saving our community from having to travel to Swan Hill to shop.'

KERRI'S TOP TIPS:

- Get lots of helpers. Ensure shareholders are willing to help out, not just say it's a good idea.
- Seek professional advice through the rural financial counselling service and other avenues available to your community.

ALISON'S TOP TIPS:

- Before opening, have a few dummy runs with pretend customers.
- If retail, have a point of sale system otherwise it's just too hard to control stock.

RICK'S TOP TIPS:

- Get at least two or three champions to generate interest in starting a coop.
- Treat it like a normal business and plan to provide a return on your investment right from the beginning.

Invest rural

Despite operating from a small outback Queensland community with a population of 367, Tambo Teddies are sold online across the world

As each annual Christmas shopping frenzy approaches, I start to see the 'Shop Local' messages circulating on social media. Of course, shopping local is great but it's not quite that simple, as every small business owner knows – especially those operating in towns where options are limited.

It is ridiculous to demonise online shopping in the midst of a digital technological revolution, especially when some of those online businesses are based locally and gaining benefit from a wider geographic audience.

Price will also be a deciding factor for many consumers and businesses seeking goods and services. Even if they do understand the multiplier effect of investing in their local community, their bank balance may dictate otherwise. Most of us have been in this position at some point in our lives, both personally and in business.

What we can do is talk about how a local business-to-business transaction could be made more achievable. Consumers have lay-by; why can't businesses agree in advance to pay off an item or negotiate a discount rather than take their custom elsewhere? It's worth considering if you have established trust.

Also, we should think carefully about how we promote our small business to the wider public. This should happen all year round, not just at Christmas.

Lately I've noticed the small independent IGA supermarket stores in rural areas displaying an A-frame notice explaining how they are part of the local community and the ways they put back into the community. Great idea. We all need to find ways to clearly articulate how we contribute to our community.

- Do we encourage our customers to talk about what goods or services they need, allowing time to source them if required?
- Do we refer customers on and promote other businesses in the local area?
- Do we lead by example and buy from other local businesses where possible?

Just to be clear. By 'local', I mean at a regional, state or national level. We are all in this together when it comes to a global economy.

Between 2016 and 2019 my work saw me travelling through rural Queensland, New South Wales and Victoria. Along the way I browsed the shops and started my Christmas shopping. I did this without guilt for my own hometown, knowing my dollars were helping make a difference to these struggling rural businesses. Their warm smiles and gratitude were obvious for all to see.

And just a point of clarification. If you don't give good service then you don't deserve anyone's custom, whether local or not. Just saying!

Every small business has the power to both attract and invest dollars wisely. I encourage you to think carefully about where your dollars will have the most impact all year round and how you can best communicate with and provide service for your customers.

An artful business

Sobrane is more than just an artist as her Broome Studio testifies

Rural Australia is becoming increasingly vibrant thanks to the artists who settle there. They are forging a lifestyle that encompasses their passion, but how do they make a living?

All too often we hear that artists are struggling and having to supplement their incomes elsewhere. Creative people are not renowned for their business acumen and yet there are many financially successful artists. If artists want to be seriously considered and earn a reasonable income, they need to apply business rigour. Difficult questions should be asked, and decisions made if they want to survive and thrive financially. How do they value an item? How do they value their time? How do they value their brand?

Apart from the works by artists of renown, who are judged by a different set of criteria, when it comes to valuing an item the old saying 'beauty is in the eye of the beholder' rings true. It is considered the most valuable to the one who admires it the most. I have never bought a piece of art without considering two things. Do I like it? And do I have a suitable space for it to be displayed? Only if the answer to those questions is yes, do I finally ask myself: Can I afford it?

So, artists first have to consider who their art will appeal to and know their price range. Central Victorian sculptor Trevor Prest's work mostly comprises of large heavy pieces most suited to big spaces. It goes without saying that an art gallery, or a company or university wanting to make an impact in their entry foyer, will pay considerably more than the average home collector. Having said that, I loved his work so much that I bought a piece and managed to squeeze it in my house.

How can an artist value their time when they are doing something they love? Like farmers who choose a lifestyle, this may be just too hard a question to answer. Perhaps a better question is to ask: What total income do you need to live comfortably? Then, it is a matter of working backwards and thinking about cash flow, what types of items bring in the best results, and how many you have to sell at what price to meet your target income. Your bestselling and most profitable items must come first. Afterwards you can indulge in your passion. As a starting base you should think about how much it costs to produce (materials, etc.), not forgetting all those small hidden costs that quickly add up, like studio rental or services, advertising, packaging and transport.

And, when it comes to the time you spend marketing your work, ensure you are spending it where it counts. An artist at a farmer's market recently told me he was about to stop selling at the markets as his items were becoming too highly priced for those attending. Good decision; he will not only save his time but also the cost of travel. Lucky I made my purchase beforehand.

Before you start thinking that I buy everything I see, I recently visited Sobrane's studio in Broome, Western Australia, and left with only a greeting card; mainly because my suitcase wasn't big enough. It was interesting to see how she has positioned herself as an artist and diversified her products to create a steady income flow. In addition to the high priced pieces for serious collectors, there were lots of smaller artworks that browsing tourists could happily purchase; for instance, cushion covers, cards and smaller unframed works. Sobrane has also embraced the latest trend of employing street artists through community grants to paint silos and other large buildings in rural communities creating tourist attractions.

Branding is king, no matter what industry you work in. If you portray yourself as a struggling artist selling whatever you can, then buyers will expect low prices. Valuing yourself and knowing the worth of your artwork is crucial in sending the right message. It all comes down to perception and how it is presented, from the sales venue right down to the look of the price tag. In the digital era with capacity for online marketing and sales, artists who create a strong brand achieve a wider reach and audience.

No businessperson has every skill required to be successful. The key is to ask the hard questions, recognise your strengths and weaknesses, seek professional advice when required, and surround yourself with a team when taking your business to the next level.

A final word of advice from someone who unfortunately doesn't have a creative bone in her body: it also helps if you're good at what you do!

The Dressmaker

Kerry introducing *The Dressmaker* under the stars in Alpha, Queensland

Viewing The Dressmaker *for the second time (on this special occasion under the stars in outback Queensland in 2016) I had the opportunity to do an introduction to the audience and reflect on what lessons could be learned from this now iconic Australian movie.*

Earlier in the day, author Rosalie Ham explained to delegates at the Isolated Children's Parents' Association meeting in Alpha how she joined a literary course at TAFE and was instructed to write a story and go through the motions of publishing it. Drawing on her somewhat skewed childhood memories of growing up in a town of 800 people with a seamstress mother, Rosalie inserted a murder, a cross-dresser, a fiercely fought football game, hate, envy, and the obligatory love story into the storyline. *The Dressmaker* was the result. Not only did it get published, it was made into a successful movie!

I first went to see the film for a number of different reasons. It was Australian and filmed in rural Victoria near where I live, plus it featured a small rural town in the storyline, albeit fictional. Most of all, it was because my mother, raised on a farm in Gippsland, was trained as a dressmaker. We went to the movie together, along with my daughter who has also inherited her grandmother's skills.

As an advocate for rural Australia I have to say that *The Dressmaker*'s depiction of Dungatar as a small town and the grating idiosyncrasies of its inhabitants was hardly ideal but we can't be too precious about that. We all understand the need for drama and humour to entertain. What I saw of value in the movie was an innovative young woman able to create her own income in a rural town, as her mother did before her.

My mother made all of our clothes. Often I was stopped by complete strangers and asked what brand my dress was. Leaving school and starting work in an office I had the snappiest wardrobe you could ever hope to have. I never thought anything of it at the time, other than it was an obvious cost saving for a rural family struggling to raise four children, pay off a mortgage, and establish an earthmoving business.

Mum's skills as a dressmaker enabled her to create a small income to support the family budget. Many a fitting for a wedding dress took place in our home with Mum threatening blue murder if we dared to go near the precious folds of white fabric. Like Rosalie who used her experiences to write *The Dressmaker*, we heard all the behind-the-scenes bridal dramas.

While I pursued a totally different career path, my daughter demonstrated skills at an early age. For her 12th birthday we gave her a second-hand sewing machine to make saddle blankets for her horses. And, as you know if you've read this book, after completing secondary college she purchased Fair Dinkum Dog Coats and began manufacturing oilskin dog coats with industrial sewing machines in her grandmother's sewing shed.

It really was lovely to see grandmother and granddaughter working together on orders to be sent Australia wide and overseas. Mum has since retired but it won't be long before the next generation, my daughter's daughters, may participate.

The moral of this story is that, whatever your skill, it can provide you with the capacity to work and live wherever you want, including in rural towns. That's what I took away from *The Dressmaker*. And, as Rosalie the author told us in Alpha: 'Rural kids are innovative, progressive and modern. They can do *anything!*'

A Call to Action

Bryce Anderson wished he'd started his business sooner

'When is it a good time to start a business?' This is the question my son asked me in 2016.

'Never' was my reply. 'Just do it!' A few months after starting his new business, Maine Plumbing, he dropped in for a coffee and admitted it was the best thing he had ever done. He only wished he had done it sooner.

Starting a new venture or buying into a business can be daunting to anyone, even if they've grown up in a small business family, as my son has. Business is a personal journey. It is your risk and your blood, sweat and tears. You can't expect anyone to guarantee a successful pathway and you can't depend on government. Quite simply it is up to you.

Sharing stories can help inspire others and give them the courage to start, to keep going, or to change direction. We can all learn from each other, which is why I love to give a voice to rural people in business.

And you don't have to be in business to help a rural entrepreneur succeed. Never underestimate the power of showing your interest and sharing a kind word at a critical moment. Be a customer! Be a partner! Be an ambassador! Maybe even an investor ...

This is about far more than providing a living for ourselves and our families in a rural context. It is also about the future of our rural towns; the need to reinvent themselves and adapt in a rapidly changing world. Entrepreneurs are the magic ingredient for every vibrant community. As so many of our leaders tell us, small business is the backbone of Australia's economy. Let us be proud of our endeavours and put a face to small businesses and entrepreneurs in every rural town to inspire others.

No matter where we live, our success – and the failures leading to that success – benefits all Australians.

Acknowledgements

First and foremost, I wish to acknowledge the amazing rural entrepreneurs and businesspeople who have generously shared their stories with me.

Images are mostly mine except where otherwise acknowledged.

A big thank you to Julie Slater for her constant advice and support, and to my family for putting up with my endless chatter about rural entrepreneurs plus long hours at a keyboard.

Finally, I want to record my appreciation to Wakefield Press for its support to Australian authors, and to the team who have made my book look fantastic.

Wakefield Press is an independent publishing and
distribution company based in Adelaide, South Australia.
We love good stories and publish beautiful books.
To see our full range of books, please visit our website at
www.wakefieldpress.com.au
where all titles are available for purchase.
To keep up with our latest releases, news and events,
subscribe to our monthly newsletter.

Find us!

Facebook: www.facebook.com/wakefield.press
Twitter: www.twitter.com/wakefieldpress
Instagram: www.instagram.com/wakefieldpress

Printed in Australia
AUHW021732070421
343644AU00001B/1

9 781743 058145